1,001 SECRETS
OF
GREAT COOKS

1,001 SECRETS
OF
GREAT COOKS

HOW TO SHOP FOR FOOD, STORE
IT, PREP IT, COOK IT, DECORATE
IT, SERVE IT AND RECYCLE IT

JEAN ANDERSON

A PERIGEE BOOK

A GENERAL ACKNOWLEDGMENT

A huge, across-the-board "thank-you" to all of my friends and fellow cooks who so graciously shared their kitchen tips for use in this collection. For a more detailed list, see the Acknowledgments at the end of the book.

A Perigee Book
Published by The Berkley Publishing Group
200 Madison Avenue
New York, NY 10016

Copyright © 1995 by Jean Anderson

Book design by Irving Perkins Associates

Cover design by Ken Salisbury.

First edition: September 1995

Published simultaneously in Canada.

Library of Congress Cataloging-in-Publication Data

1001 secrets of great cooks / [compiled by] Jean Anderson.
—1st ed.
p.   cm.
Includes index.
ISBN 0-399-52153-4 (pbk. : alk. paper)
1. Cookery—Miscellanea.   I. Anderson, Jean.
II. Title: One thousand one secrets of great cooks.   III. Title: One thousand and one secrets of great cooks.
TX652.A133   1995
641.5—dc20   95-3
                                          CIP

Printed in the United States of America
10   9   8   7   6   5   4   3   2   1

This book is printed on acid-free paper.

Contents

Contents

INTRODUCTION

Those of us who devote our lives to food—chefs, restaurateurs, cookbook authors, food writers and editors, food stylists, recipe doctors and testers, cooking school teachers, and, yes, just plain good cooks—develop, over the years, shortcuts, quick tricks, that speed and simplify everything we do with food. We learn how to zoom through supermarkets in record time, how to repackage food for maximum shelf life, how to make the most of make-aheads, how to use kitchen gadgets to best advantage, how to make food beautiful, how to entertain with grace and style.

Assembled here are 1,001 "trade secrets" graciously contributed by top food pros, food organizations and agencies, friends, and colleagues both at home and abroad.

May these "tricks of the trade" serve you as well as they've served us over the years.

A Contributors' Who's Who

Marcia Adams, cookbook author (*Marcia Adams' Heirloom Recipes: Yesterday's Favorites and Tomorrow's Treasures, Cooking from Quilt Country*); host/creator, "Marcia Adams' Kitchen," PBS Television.

Darina Allen, owner/director Ballymaloe Cookery School, Shanagarry, County Cork, Ireland; host/creator seven "Simply Delicious" cookery series, Irish Television; cookbook author (*Traditional Irish Food, Darina Allen's Simply Delicious Recipes, Festive Food of Ireland*); featured chef, BBC "Hot Chefs" series; food columnist, *Irish Times*.

Elizabeth Alston, Food Editor, *Woman's Day Magazine*; cookbook author (*Simply Cakes; Muffins; Biscuits and Scones; Tea Breads and Coffeecakes; Pancakes and Waffles*).

American Egg Board.

Frieda Arkin, cookbook author (*The Complete Book of Kitchen Wisdom*).

Janet Bailey, cookbook author (*Keeping Food Fresh*).

Beverly Barbour, Vice President Marketing, New York Restaurant Group; past President, Les Dames d'Escoffier, New York.

Ben and Karen Barker, chefs/proprietors, Magnolia Grill, Durham, North Carolina.

Nancy Verde Barr, cookbook author (*We Called It Macaroni*).

Lidia Bastianich, chef/proprietor, Felidia Restaurant, New York City; cookbook author (*La Cucina di Lidia*, with Jay Jacobs).

James Beard, cookbook author (*James Beard's New Fish Cookery, James Beard Hors D'Oeuvre and Canapés, Simple Foods, Beard on Bread, American Cookery, Delights and Prejudices*), cooking school teacher and "Godfather of American Cooking."

Simone Beck, cookbook author (*Mastering the Art of French Cooking*, with Julia Child and Louisette Bertholle, *Mastering the Art of French Cooking, Volume II*, with Julia Child, *Simca's Cuisine, Food and Friends*).

Sarah Belk, Senior Editor, *Bon Appétit Magazine*; cookbook author (*Around the Southern Table*).

Pat Bell, Travel Editor, *Gourmet Magazine*.

Bev Bennett, Food Editor, *Chicago Sun Times*; cookbook author (*Dinner for Two*).

Rose Levy Beranbaum, cookbook author (*The Cake Bible, Rose's Christmas Cookies*); cooking school teacher.

Louisette Bertholle, cookbook author (*Mastering the Art of French Cooking*, with Julia Child and Simone Beck, *French Cuisine for All*).

Marie Bianco, staff food writer, *Newsday*.

Mark Bittman, food writer; Executive Editor, *Cook's Illustrated*; cookbook author (*Fish: The Complete Guide to Buying and Cooking*).

Jean Hewitt Blair, cookbook author (*The New York Times Heritage Cookbook, The Natural Foods Cookbook*); former Food and Equipment Editor, *Family Circle*.

Flo Braker, cookbook author (*The Simple Art of Perfect Baking, Sweet Miniatures*).

Jo Ann Brett, food consultant.

Ruth Buchan, founding editor, *The Cook Book Guild*.

Marian Burros, Food News Reporter, *The New York Times*; cookbook author (*20 Minute Menus, You've Got It Made, Pure & Simple, Keep It Simple, The Elegant but Easy Cookbook*, with Lois Levine).

Jane Butel, cookbook author (*Jane Butel's Southwestern Kitchen, Hotter Than Hell, Jane Butel's Tex-Mex Cookbook, Fiesta: Southwestern Entertaining*), cooking school teacher.

California Artichoke Advisory Board.

Anna Teresa Callen, food writer; cookbook author (*Food and Memories of Abruzzo; The Wonderful World of Pizzas, Quiches and Savory Pies; Anna Teresa Callen's Menus for Pasta*); Director, Anna Teresa Callen Italian Cooking School, New York City.

Marialisa Calta, freelance food writer, syndicated food columnist.

Kathy Casey, chef/restaurant consultant.

Narcisse Chamberlain, former Senior Editor (cookbooks), William Morrow.

Laura Chenel, President, Laura Chenel's Chèvre, Inc., Sonoma, California.

Julia Child, cookbook author (*Mastering the Art of French Cooking,* with Simone Beck and Louisette Bertholle, *Mastering the Art of French Cooking, Volume II,* with Simone Beck, *Julia Child & Company, Julia Child & More Company, The Way To Cook*); television series host/creator, PBS; regular guest "Good Morning America," ABC-TV, and host, "Dishing with Julia," TV Food Network.

Bea Cihak, food consultant, *Family Circle Magazine* and *Reader's Digest General Books.*

Craig Claiborne, formerly Food Editor, *The New York Times*; author (*The New York Times Cook Book, The New York Times Menu Cook Book, Southern Cooking*).

Ann Clark, cookbook author (*Quick Cuisine*), cooking school director.

Mary Beth Clark, cookbook author; Owner/Managing Director, The International Cooking School of Italian Food and Wine, Bologna, Italy.

Whitney Clay, sous chef, Executive Dining Room, *Gourmet Magazine.*

Bernard Clayton, Jr., cookbook author (*Bernard Clayton's New Complete Book of Breads, Bernard Clayton's Cooking Across America*).

Julia della Croce, cookbook author (*The Vegetarian Table: Italy, Antipasti: The Little Dishes of Italy, Pasta Classica*), cooking teacher.

Marion Cunningham, cookbook author (*The Fannie Farmer Cookbook, The Fannie Farmer Baking Book, The Breakfast Book*).

Dolores Custer, food stylist.

Carol Cutler, cookbook author (*The Six-Minute Soufflé and Other Culinary Delights, Catch of the Day, Pâté: The New Main Course for the '80s*), syndicated columnist.

Julie Dannenbaum, cookbook author (*Fast & Fresh, Julie Dannenbaum's Creative Cooking School, Menus for All Occasions*); founder and director of Creative Cooking, Inc., Philadelphia; past director, cooking schools at the Gritti Palace Hotel in Venice, Italy, and the Greenbrier Hotel in White Sulphur Springs, West Virginia.

Lorenza de'Medici, cookbook author (*The Villa Table: 300 Classic Italian Recipes, The de'Medici Kitchen, Tuscany The Beautiful Cookbook, Florentines: A Tuscan Feast*); television series host/creator, "The de'Medici Kitchen," PBS; cooking school director.

Marcel Desaulniers, chef/co-owner, The Trellis Restaurant, Williamsburg, Virginia; cookbook author (*Death by Chocolate, The Burger Meisters*).

Cara De Silva, ethnic food writer, *New York Newsday*.

Barbara Deskins, Ph.D., R.D., Associate Professor, Clinical Dietetics and Nutrition Department, University of Pittsburgh; author (*The Nutrition Bible*, with Jean Anderson).

Jim Dodge, pastry chef, teacher, cookbook author (*Baking with Jim Dodge,* with Elaine Ratner).

Brooke Dojny, cookbook author (*Sunday Suppers, Parties, Cheap Eats,* all with Melanie Barnard), *Bon Appétit* columnist (also with Melanie Barnard).

Carol Guthrie Dovell, Food Editor, *Working Mother Magazine.*

Georgia Chan Downard, cookbook author (*The Big Broccoli Book*), food stylist.

Malachy Duffy, Senior Editor, *Food & Wine Magazine.*

Nathalie Dupree, television series host/creator, PBS; cookbook author (*Nathalie Dupree Cooks Everyday Meals from a Well-Stocked Pantry, Nathalie Dupree Cooks Great Meals for Busy Days, Nathalie Dupree's New Southern Cooking, Nathalie Dupree's Matters of Taste*).

Merle Ellis, "The Butcher."

Mary Ann Esposito, television series creator/host, "Ciao Italia," PBS; cookbook author (*Ciao Italia, Nella Cucina*).

Ben Etheridge, former cookbook consultant, *Reader's Digest Books.*

Meryle Evans, food writer, culinary historian.

Florence Fabricant, food columnist, *The New York Times*; cookbook author (*Florence Fabricant's Pleasures of the Table, New Home Cooking*).

Barbara Fairchild, Executive Editor, *Bon Appetit Magazine.*

Carol Field, cookbook author (*The Italian Baker, Celebrating Italy, Italy in Small Bites*).

Jim Fobel, cookbook author (*Big Flavors*).

Larry Forgione, chef/proprietor, An American Place, New York City, and The Beekman Tavern, Rhinebeck, NY.

Lee Fowler, cookbook consultant, *Reader's Digest Books*.

Jean Todd Freeman, freelance writer, former Associate Editor, *Ladies' Home Journal*.

Susan Friedland, Senior Editor, HarperCollins Publishers.

Betty Fussell, culinary historian, food writer/author (*The Story of Corn, I Hear America Cooking*).

Gilroy's Finest Garlic.

Sandra Rose Gluck, cookbook author (*The Best of Coffee, The Best of the Mediterranean,* and *From the Farmer's Market,* with Richard Sax), recipe developer.

Rozanne Gold, cookbook author (*Little Meals*), Culinary Director, Joseph Baum & Michael Whiteman Company (Rainbow Room, Windows on the World), New York City.

Gary A. Goldberg, Executive Director, Culinary Arts at The New School, New York City.

Joyce Goldstein, cookbook author (*Joyce Goldstein's Mediterranean: The Beautiful Cookbook, The Mediterranean Kitchen, Back to Square One*), chef/proprietor Square One Restaurant, San Francisco.

Bert Greene, cooking teacher, television chef, cookbook author (*Bert Greene's Kitchen Bouquets, Greene on Greens, The Grains Cookbook*).

Gael Greene, restaurant critic, *New York Magazine*.

Dotty Griffith, Food Editor, *Dallas Morning News*.

Linda and Fred Griffith, cookbook authors (*Onions, Onions,*

Onions; The New American Farm Cookbook; The Best of the Midwest). Fred Griffith is host of the daily television show "The Morning Exchange," WEWS-TV, Cleveland.

Michel Guérard, chef/proprietor Les Prés d'Eugénie, Eugénie-les-Bains, France; cookbook author (*Michel Guérard's Cuisine Minceur, Michel Guérard's Cuisine Gourmand*).

Carol Haddix, Food Guide Editor, *Chicago Tribune*; editor, three recent *Chicago Tribune* cookbooks.

Ken Haedrich, cookbook author (*Ken Haedrich's Country Baking*).

Zack Hanle, Editor-at-Large, *Bon Appétit Magazine*.

Elaine Hanna, cookbook author (*The New Doubleday Cookbook* and *Micro Ways*, both with Jean Anderson), former Food Editor, *Ladies' Home Journal*.

Margaret Happel, Food and Nutrition Editor, *Redbook Magazine*.

Alan Harding, chef, Nosmo King Restaurant, New York City.

Jessica B. Harris, culinary historian, cookbook author (*The Welcome Table: African-American Heritage Cooking—A Feast of Over 200 Recipes from All Over the Country; Tasting Brazil; Sky Juice and Fly Fish*).

Nao Hauser, food writer.

Joanne Lamb Hayes, Food Editor, *Country Living Magazine*; cookbook author (*365 Great Cookies & Brownies, Rice, The Weekend Kitchen*, all with Bonnie Tandy Leblang).

Marcella Hazan, international teacher of Italian cooking, cookbook author (*Essentials of Classic Italian Cooking,*

Marcella's Italian Kitchen, More Classic Italian Cooking, The Classic Italian Cook Book).

Jan T. Hazard, Food and Equipment Editor, *Ladies' Home Journal.*

Ken Hom, cookbook author (*Asian Vegetarian Feast, Ken Hom's Quick & Easy Chinese Cooking*), television chef.

JA (Jean Anderson).

Dana Jacobi, food writer.

Dora Jonassen, food stylist.

Barbara Kafka, cookbook author (*The Microwave Gourmet, Party Food, The Opinionated Palate*); columnist, *Gourmet Magazine*; regular guest, TV Food Network.

Katharine Kagel, chef/proprietor, Cafe Pasqual's, Santa Fe, New Mexico; cookbook author (*Cafe Pasqual's Cookbook*).

Madeleine Kamman, Director, School for American Chefs, Beringer Vineyards, St. Helena, California; cookbook author (*Madeleine Cooks, In Madeleine's Kitchen, Madeleine Kamman's Savoie, When French Women Cook*); television series host, "Madeleine Cooks," PBS.

Lynne Rossetto Kasper, cookbook author (*The Splendid Table: Recipes from Emilia-Romagna, the Heartland of Northern Italian Food*).

Peggy Katalinich, Food Editor, *Family Circle Magazine.*

Thomas Keller, chef/proprietor, The French Laundry, Yountville, California.

Diana Kennedy, cookbook author (*Mexican Regional Cooking, The Cuisines of Mexico, The Art of Mexican Cooking*), culinary historian and teacher of Mexican cooking.

Graham Kerr, international culinary consultant; television series host, "Graham Kerr's Kitchen," PBS, and "The Graham Kerr Show," Discovery; cookbook author (*Graham Kerr's Kitchen, Graham Kerr's Creative Choices Cookbook, Graham Kerr's Smart Cooking*).

Johanne Killeen and **George Germon,** chefs/proprietors, Al Forno Restaurant, Providence, Rhode Island; cookbook authors (*Cucina Simpatica*).

Jane Kirby, Editor-in-Chief, *Eating Well Magazine.*

Peter Kump, President, Peter Kump's New York Cooking School; President, The James Beard Foundation.

Gray Kunz, Chef de Cuisine, Restaurant Lespinasse, New York City.

Emeril Lagasse, chef/proprietor, Emeril's Restaurant, New Orleans; cooking show host, TV Food Network; cookbook author (*Emeril's New New Orleans Cooking,* with Jessie Tirsch).

Carole Lalli, cookbook author (*Chicken Salads*); Senior Editor, Rizzoli International; former Editor-in-Chief, *Food & Wine Magazine.*

Linda Romanelli Leahy, cookbook author (*The World's Greatest Peanut Butter Cookbook,* with Jack Maguire), teacher, food writer.

Bonnie Tandy LeBlang, syndicated food columnist, cookbook author (*365 Great Cookies & Brownies, Rice, The Weekend Kitchen,* all with Joanne Hayes, and *Country Entertaining*).

Jeanne Lesem, cookbook author (*Preserving Today*).

Faye Levy, cookbook author (*Faye Levy's International Jewish Cookbook, Faye Levy's International Vegetable Cookbook*).

Florence S. Lin, cookbook author (*Florence Lin's Book of Chinese Noodles, Dumplings and Breads; Chinese One-Dish Dinners; Florence Lin's Chinese Vegetarian Cookbook*), teacher of Chinese cooking.

Eileen Yin-Fei Lo, cookbook author (*From the Earth: Chinese Vegetarian Cooking*), cooking teacher, China Institute of America, New York City.

Lori Longbotham, food writer, recipe developer, cookbook author (*Better by Microwave*, with Marie Simmons).

Dione Lucas, cooking school teacher, television chef, cookbook author (*The Dione Lucas Book of French Cooking*, with Marion Gorman).

Sheila Lukins, cookbook author (*The New Basics Cookbook* and *The Silver Palate Cookbook*, both with Julee Rosso, and *Sheila Lukins All Around the World Cookbook*).

Mary Lyons, former Director, Public Relations, Food and Wines from France.

Deborah Madison, chef, restaurant consultant, cookbook author (*The Greens Cookbook*, with Edward Espe Brown, and *The Savory Way*).

Nick Malgieri, Director, Baking Program, Peter Kump's New York Cooking School, cookbook author (*Perfect Pastry, Great Italian Desserts*).

John Mariani, author (*The Dictionary of American Food & Drink, America Eats Out*).

Priscilla Martel, chef/food consultant.

Michael McLaughlin, cookbook author (*The Mushroom*

Book, Fifty-Two Meat Loaves, The New American Kitchen, The Back of the Box Gourmet, More Back of the Box Gourmet).

Alice Medrich, cookbook author (*Cocolat: Extraordinary Chocolate Desserts, The Art of Low-Fat Desserts*).

Danny Meyer, New York restaurateur (Union Square Cafe, Gramercy Tavern), cookbook author (*The Union Square Cafe Cookbook,* with Michael Romano, chef).

Bryan Miller, food/feature writer, *The New York Times.*

Kemp Minifie, Senior Food Editor, *Gourmet Magazine.*

Deborah Mintcheff, food stylist.

Pamela Mitchell, Associate Food Editor, *Food & Wine Magazine.*

Sara Moulton, Executive Chef, *Gourmet Magazine.*

Joan Nathan, cookbook author (*Jewish Cooking in America*).

Cornelius O'Donnell, cookbook author/editor (*Designed for Living: Quick, Healthy and Delicious Recipes; Cooking with Cornelius: The Corning Cookbook*), food columnist.

Beatrice Ojakangas, home economist, food writer, cookbook author (*Beatrice Ojakangas' Great Holiday Baking Book, The Great Scandinavian Baking Book, The Book of Regional American Cooking: Heartland*).

Jacques Pépin, cookbook author (*Happy Cooking, Simple and Healthy Cooking, The Short-Cut Cook, A French Chef Cooks at Home, La Technique, La Méthode*), teacher, television series host, "Today's Gourmet," PBS.

James Peterson, cookbook author (*Sauces, Splendid Soups*), cooking teacher.

Earl Peyroux, television series host/chef, "Gourmet Cooking," WSRE-TV, Pensacola, FL.

Charles Pierce, cookbook author/editor (*365 Ways To Cook Fish and Shellfish, The New Settlement Cookbook, Southern Light Cooking*).

Paul Prudhomme, chef/proprietor, K-Paul's, New Orleans; cookbook author (*Chef Paul Prudhomme's Louisiana Kitchen, The Prudhomme Family Cookbook, Chef Paul Prudhomme's Seasoned America, Chef Paul Prudhomme's Fork in the Road,* and *Chef Paul's Pure Magic*).

Wolfgang Puck, chef/proprietor, Spago, Los Angeles; television chef; cookbook author (*Adventures in the Kitchen, The Wolfgang Puck Cookbook*).

Steven Raichlen, syndicated food columnist; Director, Cooking in Paradise Cooking School, Saint Barthélemy, French West Indies; cookbook author (*Miami Spice, Steven Raichlen's High-Flavor, Low-Fat Cooking*).

Guy Reuge, chef/proprietor, Mirabelle Restaurant, St. James, New York.

Michael Roberts, chef, cookbook author (*Secret Ingredients, What's for Dinner?*).

Betty Rosbottom, food writer, syndicated food columnist, cooking teacher, cookbook author (*Betty Rosbottom's Cooking School Cookbook, First Impressions*).

Elisabeth Rozin, cookbook author (*Ethnic Cuisine, Blue Corn and Chocolate*).

Shirley Sarvis, food and wine writer/consultant.

Irene Sax, Food Editor, *Newsday, New York Newsday*.

Richard Sax, food writer; columnist (with Marie Simmons), *Bon Appétit Magazine*; cookbook author (*Classic Home Desserts*).

Elizabeth Schneider, produce specialist; food writer; contributor, *Food Arts Magazine, Eating Well Magazine;* cookbook author (*Uncommon Fruits & Vegetables: A Commonsense Guide*).

Sally Schneider, cookbook author (*The Art of Low-Calorie Cooking*).

Dieter G. Schorner, pastry chef, Patisserie Café Didier, Washington, DC.

Natalie Schram, former editor, *Bon Appétit Magazine.*

Regina Schrambling, magazine food writer, cookbook author (*Squash: A Country Garden Cookbook*).

Arthur Schwartz, New York City radio food show host, restaurant critic, cookbook author (*Soup Suppers, What to Cook*).

Michele Scicolone, food writer, teacher, cookbook author (*The Antipasto Table, La Dolce Vita*).

Judith Segal, cook extraordinaire.

Nancy Silverton, pastry chef, proprietor (with Mark Peel), Campanile Restaurant, Los Angeles; cookbook author (*Mark Peel & Nancy Silverton at Home: Two Chefs Cook for Family and Friends*, with Mark Peel, and *Desserts*).

Marie Simmons, syndicated food columnist; co-columnist (with Richard Sax), *Bon Appétit Magazine;* cookbook author (*Bar Cookies A to Z; The Light Touch Cookbook; Italian Light Cooking; Rice, The Amazing Grain;* and *Better by Microwave*, with Lori Longbotham).

Thelma K. Snyder, author (with Marcia Cone) of six microwave cookbooks.

Marlene Sorosky, cookbook author (*Marlene Sorosky's Cooking for Holidays and Celebrations, The Dessert Lover's Cookbook, Easy Entertaining with Marlene Sorosky*), cooking teacher.

Lyn Stallworth, food writer, cookbook author (*The Country Fair Cookbook, The Brooklyn Cookbook*, both with Rod Kennedy, Jr.).

Leah Stewart, food consultant.

Martha Stewart, cookbook author (*Martha Stewart's Menus for Entertaining, Entertaining*); founding editor, *Martha Stewart Living*; syndicated television series host/creator, "Martha Stewart Living."

Diana Sturgis, Test Kitchen Director, *Food & Wine Magazine*.

Elizabeth Terry, chef/proprietor, Elizabeth on 37th, Savannah, Georgia.

Barbara Tropp, chef/proprietor, China Moon Cafe, San Francisco; cookbook author (*China Moon Cookbook, The Modern Art of Chinese Cooking*).

Jack Ubaldi, cookbook author (*Jack Ubaldi's Meat Book*, with Elizabeth Crossman).

Tina Ujlaki, Food Editor, *Food & Wine Magazine*.

Michele Urvater, cookbook author (*Monday-to-Friday Pasta, Monday-to-Friday Cookbook*), television series host, "How To Feed Your Family on $99 a Week," TV Food Network.

James Villas, Food and Wine Editor, *Town & Country Magazine*; cookbook author (*My Mother's Southern Kitchen*, with

Martha Pearl Villas; *American Taste*; *The French Country Kitchen*).

Jeanne Voltz, food writer; cookbook author (*The Florida Cookbook*, with Caroline Stuart; *Barbecued Ribs, Smoked Butts, and Other Great Feeds*; *The Flavor of the South*); former Food Editor, *Woman's Day Magazine* and *The Los Angeles Times*.

Carole Walter, cookbook author (*Great Cakes*).

Alice Waters, chef/proprietor, Chez Panisse, Berkeley, California; cookbook author (*The Chez Panisse Menu Cookbook, Fanny at Chez Panisse*, with Bob Carrau and Patricia Curtan).

William Woys Weaver, culinary historian, cookbook author (*America Eats, Pennsylvania Dutch Country Cooking*).

Jan Weimer, food writer, food consultant.

Connie Welch, food and nutrition consultant.

Patricia Wells, restaurant critic, food writer, cookbook author (*The Food Lover's Guide to Paris, The Food Lover's Guide to France, Bistro Cooking, Patricia Wells' Trattoria*).

Jasper White, chef/proprietor, Jasper's, Boston; cookbook author (*Jasper White's Cooking from New England*).

Anne Willan, founder, *Ecole de Cuisine la Varenne*, Paris; director of teaching programs at Château du Fey, Burgundy, and The Greenbrier, White Sulphur Springs, West Virginia; cookbook author (*France Gastronomique, La Varenne Practique, Anne Willan's Look & Cook* series); television series host/creator, "Anne Willan's Look & Cook," PBS.

Lucy Wing, food editor, writer, consultant; cookbook editor (*Country Mornings, Country Baker*).

Helen Witty, food writer/editor, cookbook author (*Fancy Pantry, Mrs. Witty's Monster Cookies, Mrs. Witty's Home-Style Menu Cookbook*).

Paula Wolfert, cookbook author (*The Cooking of the Eastern Mediterranean, Paula Wolfert's World of Food, Couscous and Other Good Food from Morocco*).

Rita Wolfson, food editor/writer.

Hedy Würz, cookbook author (*The New German Cookbook,* with Jean Anderson).

Martin Yan, PBS television series host, "Yan Can Cook," cookbook author (*Everybody's Wokking, The Yan Can Cook Book*).

Zanne Early Zakroff, Executive Food Editor, *Gourmet Magazine.*

SHOPPING

1. To avoid last-minute shopping and having to make decisions under pressure, plan family menus a week in advance.

—Jan T. Hazard

2. Make your own permanent shopping list of all the groceries you buy regularly, leaving space for write-ins. Run off lots of copies and post one, with pencil attached, on the refrigerator or cupboard door so you and other family members can check needed items as they run low. When you head for the store with one completed list, tape up a new one.

—Marcia Adams,
Elizabeth Alston

3. When making a shopping list, group items according to the floorplan of your supermarket. Start with the first section you'll come to (usually produce) and continue, keeping all dairy products together, all beans and grains, etc. This way you'll be less likely to forget items.

—Steven Raichlen

1

4. Always buy frozen foods last. That way they're less likely to thaw before you get them home.

—JA

5. Shop with cupboards, fridge, and freezer space in mind, buying only what you can store without waste.

—*Conventional kitchen wisdom*

6. Consider these frozen foods staples—artichoke hearts, baby lima beans, whole-kernel corn, cooked puréed winter squash, chopped spinach, sliced peaches, whole berries (especially blueberries, raspberries, and strawberries), pie crusts (both standard and deep dish), puff pastry, and filo leaves. They're as good as the fresh and a tremendous convenience.

—LEAH STEWART

7. When you set out for the produce market or expect to visit several shops, take along a couple of sturdy paper shopping bags with strong handles, folded up and tucked in your shoulder bag. They're great for loading with small purchases and stand up better than plastic in your car, the bus, or commuter train.

—DIANA STURGIS

8. Shopping for exotic foods not available in your supermarket can take time, so before you head for a specialty food shop, check the pantry and see what you're missing. At the store, look around, read labels, ask questions. Keeping unusual ingredients on hand will give you the flexibility to try out new ideas.

—ELISABETH ROZIN

9. You can save money by planning for leftovers. For example, when shopping for a special dinner, make sure you buy enough for seconds, then freeze the leftovers for another meal.

—ZACK HANLE

10. Baking powder goes flat fairly fast, so buy it in small tins.

—JIM DODGE, adapted from
Baking with Jim Dodge, with
Elaine Ratner (Simon &
Schuster)

11. To make sure you're getting the very freshest spices, buy them in bulk in tiny bags once a month at a busy health food shop.

—ELIZABETH TERRY

12. You'll save kitchen time (if not money) by buying a selection of already-cut-up vegetables from your store's salad bar.

—MARIAN BURROS

13. Stock up on condiments to press into duty at a moment's notice—beer mustard from Wisconsin, Dijon from France, mustards flavored with green peppercorns or hot chilies. All add zip to sauces or salad dressings and are terrific spread on chicken or fish before baking.

—PEGGY KATALINICH

14. Flavored barbecue sauces, especially honey-mustard blends, are great to keep on hand. Korean barbecue sauce, straight off the supermarket shelf, is a pungent seasoning that adds a lot of flavor with very little effort.

—PEGGY KATALINICH

15. When selecting an olive oil, consider its use. "Extra virgin" is best for salad dressing or pasta; for greasing pans, the cheaper "pure" is plenty good enough.

—LEAH STEWART

16. A good artichoke will talk to you. This means that when fresh, it will squeak when lightly handled (but when oversqueaked, it will bruise).

—JULIA CHILD

17. Fresh broccoli doesn't smell; if it does, pass it by.

—BERT GREENE, adapted from
The Vegetable Lover's Video
(Videocraft Classics, NYC)

18. The juiciest citrus fruits are the heavy ones with firm, fresh rind.

—TINA UJLAKI

19. The larger the lime, the more it looks like a lemon, the sweeter it will be. Tiny limes, especially round ones, will be mouth-puckeringly tart—like the famous Key limes of Florida.

—JA

20. Before buying a bunch of grapes, shake it gently. If the grapes cling to their stems, they're fresh; if they fall off, they're past their prime.

—*Conventional kitchen wisdom*

21. When buying fresh peppers to roast, choose those that are a little wrinkled but still unblemished. Wrinkling indicates maturity [mellowness].

—ANNA TERESA CALLEN

22. Buy dried hot red peppers (sweet and tepid *anchos*, fiery *cayennes*, or explosive *habaneros*) and grind your own chili powder in an electric blender or food processor. For small amounts use a little electric coffee grinder. But don't inhale the fumes.

—JA

23. Choose potatoes about the same size, so they'll cook at the same rate and won't have to be removed at different times. If you buy thin-skinned reds and whites, you don't need to peel them—just give them a quick scrub and steam them to hold in nutrients.

—DIANA STURGIS

24. When buying acorn, butternut, or other winter squash, choose those with dull skin. Shiny skin means the squash was probably picked green.

—JANET BAILEY, adapted from
Keeping Food Fresh
(HarperCollins)

25. Don't waste money on shriveled dry vanilla beans. Only the plump, moist ones will have proper flavor.

—NANCY SILVERTON, adapted from
Desserts (HarperCollins)

26. When buying half a ham, go for the butt end. It's meatier than the shank end.

—JA

27. If steaks (porterhouse and T-bones) are on special and priced the same per pound, choose the porterhouse. It's got more tenderloin than the T-bone.

—JA

28. Want bargain mini pot roasts? Buy cross-cut beef shanks.

—JA

29. The bigger the turkey, the more meat you'll get per pound.

—JA

30. Always taste nuts before buying to make sure they haven't gone rancid.

—JOYCE GOLDSTEIN

31. Buy raw nuts in large quantities and store them in the freezer. Toast them a pound at a time so they're always ready for baking or nibbling.

—JAN T. HAZARD

32. When shopping for whole-grain breads, rely on labels instead of appearance. A rich brown color may simply mean that molasses has been added.

—GRAHAM KERR, adapted from
Graham Kerr's Smart Cooking
(Doubleday)

33. Never waste money on "cooking" sherry. It's salted. Always buy the wines you cook with as carefully as you buy the wines you drink—they're one and the same.

—*Conventional kitchen wisdom*

34. Cordials and liqueurs often cost the earth. So if you need only an ounce or two for a recipe, buy a "mini."

—*Conventional kitchen wisdom*

35. At the checkout counter, practice "destination bagging." Ask the clerk to put (or do it yourself) perishables destined for the refrigerator in one bag, canned foods for the pantry in another, club soda and tonic for the bar in still another. Bag freezer foods separately and put them in your car last so they'll be unloaded first.

—CORNELIUS O'DONNELL

36. When you come home from the store with items that need special preparation before storing, like fresh garlic and bell peppers, save time and later trouble by starting the preparation process while you're putting away the rest of your groceries.

—CORNELIUS O'DONNELL

37. Sleuth flea markets and tag sales for pie pans with holes in the bottom (they ensure crisp bottom crusts) and plastic lazy-Susans (just the thing to hold a cake while you frost it).

—LEAH STEWART

STORAGE

Pantry, Fridge, Freezer

38. Keep your pantry well stocked with convenience foods (canned, bottled, freeze-dried) and enhance them with your own special touches—for example, add sautéed fresh mushrooms to ready-to-heat pasta sauces.

—ZACK HANLE

39. Before shelving unusual or exotic foods (dried mushrooms, chilies, flours, etc.), especially those you've bought in ethnic shops or while traveling, "quarantine" them in your freezer for 48 hours to kill any invisible fauna (tiny insects, insect eggs, etc.) that might be present.

—ZANNE ZAKROFF

40. Use masking tape or pressure-sensitive labels (stationery stores stock them in all shapes, sizes, and colors) to label jars of staples (flours, grains, dried beans, lentils, etc.). They stick, but pull off neatly when an empty jar is pressed into service for storing something else.

—JA

41. Use half-gallon preserving jars for storing pastas, grains, sugars, flours, dried beans, peas, and lentils. They keep "livestock" at bay—both from entering the jar or from escaping should weevil eggs in a flour or grain hatch.

—JA

AND

42. Don't forget to label the jars and include cooking instructions, if needed. [Often you can cut these right off the package and tuck them inside the jar. —JA]

—BEATRICE OJAKANGAS

43. To seal storage jars or cannisters airtight, wrap a strip of masking tape or strapping tape around the closure.

—DANA JACOBI

44. Label dried herbs with the date of purchase and store on a cool, dark, dry shelf. Sniff every six months and when they smell stale and grassy, replenish.

—*Conventional kitchen wisdom*

45. Store opened boxes of food in self-sealing plastic bags to keep their ingredients fresh. Raisins and dried currants will stay moist, potato flakes and cornstarch, etc., will stay dry.

—BEATRICE OJAKANGAS

46. Seal small amounts of ingredients (nuts, wild rice, lentils, raisins, etc.) in plastic sandwich bags, then store all the little bags in a single cannister.

—BEATRICE OJAKANGAS

47. Store olive oil, herbs, and spices away from sunlight. They'll keep better.

—JOYCE GOLDSTEIN

48. Always store baking powder and baking soda on a cool, dry shelf to keep them active as long as possible. Once baking soda has lost its punch, use it in the refrigerator or freezer to absorb odors.

—JA

49. Yeast will keep longer if stored in screw-top glass jars in the freezer.

—*Conventional kitchen wisdom*

50. To keep brown sugar moist, store in an airtight container with a whole orange, lemon, or lime.

—DIONE LUCAS, adapted from *The
Dione Lucas Book of French
Cooking,* with Marion Gorman
(Little, Brown)

OR

51. Store brown sugar in a tightly covered cannister with a slice of apple or bread.

—*Conventional kitchen wisdom*

OR

52. The first time you open a box of brown sugar, cut across the top of the inside bag with scissors. Take out what you need, roll the top down, pressing out as much air as you can, and staple it shut with three to four staples at the top. (Caution: Be careful not to drop a staple in the sugar!) For good measure, put the stapled bag in another plastic bag. Stored like this, brown sugar will stay moist forever.

—MICHELE URVATER

OR

53. Slip a strip of orange rind into the plastic bag of sugar, twist the bag shut, and replace it in the box *upside down.*

—JIM FOBEL

54. Imported black Gaeta olives—great for sprinkling on pizza or tossing into pasta—can be stored in glass jars either in their own brine or under olive oil.

—NANCY VERDE BARR

55. Keep chickpea flour in the pantry to make a quick and simple soup—"fournade"—an easy blend of chickpea flour, water, olive oil, and *quatre épices* (a commercial spice blend) to taste.

—ROZANNE GOLD

56. With tomato paste and anchovy paste in the refrigerator, it's easy to perk up lackluster soups and stews.

—PEGGY KATALINICH

12

57. Keep a jar of sun-dried tomatoes in your cupboard, then purée and spread on fish or chicken before broiling. Or use as the base of a tomato and sweet-red-pepper sauce.

—PEGGY KATALINICH

58. If dried chili peppers are to keep their fresh, shiny color, they must be refrigerated. Crushed red peppers have a shelf life of about two years. Discard any dried peppers that have turned dark red or cloudy, they may be harsh and bitter.

—PATRICIA WELLS, adapted from *Patricia Wells' Trattoria* (William Morrow)

59. Store grated chocolate in the freezer to use in tempering; frozen chocolate works faster and you can scoop out just what you need.

—THOMAS KELLER

60. Never store chocolate in plastic wrap—it gives chocolate an unpleasant taste. Wrap it instead in freezer paper, then overwrap in foil. And keep it moisture free by storing in a dark, cool, dry place away from strong odors (like onion).

—JIM DODGE, adapted from *Baking with Jim Dodge*, with Elaine Ratner (Simon & Schuster)

61. After using vanilla beans for flavoring, dry them well with paper towels and bury them in a cannister of

sugar (granulated or confectioners'). This will flavor the sugar while preserving the beans for several more uses.

—CHARLES PIERCE

62. If you frequently use only one slice of bacon at a time (for flavoring chowder, for example), try this convenient trick. Fold each bacon strip in half and wrap individually in plastic wrap, then bundle all wrapped slices in a plastic bag, seal, and freeze. This way you can remove as many single slices as you need.

—RUTH BUCHAN

63. When you bring meat home from the store, unwrap, place on a plate, cover loosely with plastic food wrap, and store in the coldest part of the refrigerator. To discourage bacterial growth, meat needs to breathe.

—*Conventional kitchen wisdom*

64. If you intend to keep broth or stock in the refrigerator for several days, don't skim off the fat; it helps seal out germs and other microorganisms.

—*Conventional kitchen wisdom*

65. After buying fresh oysters or clams in the shell, let them chill in the freezer for an hour or longer to make them easier to shuck or open.

—ZACK HANLE

66. To refresh fish that's gotten sticky on the way home from the store, use this ancient Scottish crofter's

trick called "crimping": Add sea salt to cold water, about 1 tablespoon for 2 quarts. Drop in enough ice cubes to plummet the temperature to North Sea levels, slip your fish directly into the iced "sea water," and leave it there about 15 minutes. When you dry it off, give it a sniff. It should smell sea-sweet.

—GRAHAM KERR, adapted from
Graham Kerr's Smart Cooking
(Doubleday)

67. After buying fresh fish, place it in the refrigerator between self-sealing plastic bags filled with ice cubes. This will keep the fish from getting soggy.

—ELIZABETH TERRY

68. Keeping shellfish fresh can be tricky. Crabs and lobsters will keep an extra day or two wrapped in *damp* newspapers and stored in the refrigerator. Bivalves such as oysters, clams, and mussels should be wrapped very tightly in a mesh or otherwise perforated bag, *firmly weighted down* and put in the fridge. This method, by preventing them from opening and spilling their juices, maintains their quality and extends their life.

—JASPER WHITE

69. Cover fresh shrimp completely with water and freeze in plastic containers. When thawed under cold running water and cooked, they will taste like fresh.

—JAMES VILLAS

70. Dairy products (milk, yogurt, cream, etc.) will keep twice as long if you transfer them from cartons to screw-top glass jars before refrigerating.

—ANN CLARK

71. To keep Cheddar, Swiss, and other firm cheeses from drying, rub soft butter over the cut surfaces, over-wrap in plastic food wrap, and store in the refrigerator.

—*Conventional kitchen wisdom*

72. To keep Parmesan cheese fresh, wrap first in slightly dampened paper towels, then in a damp cloth towel or cheesecloth, and store in the refrigerator.

—JULIA DELLA CROCE, adapted from *Pasta Classica* (Chronicle)

OR

73. Buy a chunk of Parmesan only large enough to last about a month, grate it into a jar, seal tight, refrigerate, and have ready for omelettes, sauces, gratins, and salads.

—JAMES VILLAS

OR

74. Grate Parmesan and other hard cheeses in a food processor, transfer to a self-sealing plastic bag, and freeze. Grated cheese keeps better in the freezer than in the refrigerator.

—JULIA DELLA CROCE

75. Extend the life of *chèvre* by placing in a little ceramic bowl, covering with olive oil then plastic food wrap, and storing in the refrigerator.

—JA

76. Cottage cheese and yogurt will stay fresh longer if the cartons are stored upside down. Just make sure the lids don't leak.

—*Conventional kitchen wisdom*

77. Store eggs in their own carton on a refrigerator shelf, not in the egg-holders set into the door itself. They'll last longer. Opening and closing the door not only exposes eggs to fluctuations of temperature but also increases the risk of breakage.

—AMERICAN EGG BOARD

78. Pencil an "X" on hard-boiled eggs to distinguish them from raw eggs if both are stored together in the refrigerator.

—PATRICIA BELL

79. For transporting deviled eggs, fill one plastic bag with egg yolk filling mixture, the other with hard-boiled white halves, and place both on ice. Fill the eggs on location.

—AMERICAN EGG BOARD

80. Fruit will keep better if you don't wash it until just before serving.

—JOYCE GOLDSTEIN

81. Always unband asparagus spears, broccoli, arugula, romaine, and other greens before storing. Tuck into self-sealing plastic bags along with several sheets of paper toweling to absorb excess moisture and store in the fridge. If the bands are left on, vegetables will wilt and spoil twice as fast.

—JA

82. And here's a variation on "the best possible way to store asparagus." Unwrap the asparagus and slice ½ inch off the butt end of each stalk. Submerge stalks in a bowl of warm water and let "refresh" 30 minutes. Place 2 inches water in a 1-quart measuring cup; stand asparagus in the cup, butt ends down; pop a plastic bag over the asparagus tips, leaving it loose; and store in fridge. This way asparagus will keep fresh two to three days.

—JULIA CHILD, adapted from *Julia Child & More Company* (Knopf)

AND

83. If you change the water every three to four days, the asparagus will keep fresh for as long as two weeks.

—JAMES VILLAS

84. Lay plastic wrap directly on the surface of guacamole or pesto to seal out the air and keep them from discoloring. Use the same method to keep skin from forming on sauces and puddings.

—LYN STALLWORTH

85. If you stand broccoli bouquet style in a jar of cool water and pop a plastic bag over the top, it should last a week or more in the fridge.

—BERT GREENE, adapted from
The Vegetable Lover's Video
(Videocraft Classics)

86. When using only part of a cucumber, tomato, or apple, place the remainder, unpeeled and cut side down, on a flat, opaque plate (clear glass exposes the food to light). This technique not only preserves the food but also saves on storage wraps.

—PAMELA MITCHELL

87. Peeled garlic cloves, submerged in wine, can be safely stored in the refrigerator and used as long as no mold or yeast appears on the surface of the wine.

—GILROY'S FINEST GARLIC

88. Put a whole head of garlic under a dish towel and hit it with a heavy pot. The cloves will separate and the skins loosen so that you can easily remove them. Cut off root end of each clove, chop all the garlic, wrap tightly in plastic wrap, seal inside a self-sealing plastic bag, and store in the coldest part of the refrigerator. Use within a week or two.

—BARBARA KAFKA

89. Garlic covered in oil should always be stored in a covered container in the coldest part of the refrigerator

and kept in small amounts—make only as much as you will use in two weeks. *These precautions are necessary to eliminate the risk of botulism toxin, produced in the absence of oxygen, at temperatures above 50° F.* Storing fresh garlic in oil is a widely practiced custom and is perfectly safe as long as you observe these precautions.

—GILROY'S FINEST GARLIC

90. Storing chopped garlic in olive oil in your refrigerator counteracts food odors while keeping the garlic fresh.

—GRAY KUNZ

91. Refrigerate mushrooms and eggplant in paper rather than plastic bags to keep them from developing soft, slimy spots.

—JOYCE GOLDSTEIN

92. For maximum flavor and long life, wrap prized onions (like Vidalias) individually in newspaper and store in a cool, dark place.

—JAMES VILLAS

93. Before storing scallions, parsley, or cilantro in the refrigerator, air-dry them quickly in front of a fan to minimize wilting. Then store in a plastic bag.

—JIM FOBEL

And

94. Unless parsley is very young, remove stems. Then chop and store in the refrigerator in a perforated plastic bag. The parsley will remain fresh for about a week.

—Julia della Croce

95. If you're in for a week of heavy-duty cooking, chop batches of onions and sweet peppers, triple-bag separately in self-sealing plastic bags, and store in the refrigerator. Then whenever you need chopped onions or chopped peppers, just scoop out what you need. NOTE: These chopped-ahead vegetables should be reserved for recipes that will be cooked.

—JA

Also

96. Chop a bunch of parsley ahead of time. Roll in dampened paper toweling, overwrap in dry paper toweling, then tuck inside a self-sealing plastic bag, and store in the refrigerator. It will keep fresh for about a week.

—JA

97. The absolutely foolproof way to store fresh basil, chervil, cilantro, parsley, tarragon, and other delicate herbs: Pretend you're arranging long-stemmed roses. Lay each herb stalk gently on its side and slice the stem end off, holding the knife on the bias. Strip off any wilted leaves. Half fill an iced-tea glass or pint pre-

serving jar with water, mix in a pinch of sugar, stand the herbs in the water, and pop a plastic bag upside down—*loosely*—over the herbs. Stored in the refrigerator this way, delicate herbs will keep fresh and aromatic for a week or more.

—JA

98. As soon as you bring cilantro home from the market, stand it upright in a glass of warm water to give it a final drink, then wrap a wet paper towel around its roots (it will last longer with roots intact). Place in plastic bag and store in the refrigerator for 3 to 4 days maximum. Do not rinse until just before using, then rinse well.

—JIM FOBEL

99. To keep fresh herbs fresh, remember that they like carbon dioxide. So put them in a plastic bag, blow air into the bag as if it were a balloon, and seal it tight.

—BETTY FUSSELL

100. Basil leaves are fragile and turn brown quickly. Keep them on short stems, rinse and dry gently, layer between paper towels enclosed in a large plastic bag with air trapped inside, and refrigerate.

—LUCY WING

101. Still another way to preserve fresh herbs: First spread a thin layer of kosher salt in a rectangular plastic container. Over this, place a single layer of herbs (this method is best suited for basil, sage, and mint),

another light layer of salt, and so on, until you've covered all the herb leaves. Cover, label and store the container in the pantry until needed. Then gently remove the salt to expose the herbs, which will be darkened but still soft and full of fragrance and flavor.

—EARL PEYROUX

102. Pluck bunches of flat-leaved parsley clean, then wash, spin dry, and store in a self-sealing plastic bag in the refrigerator.

—KEMP MINIFIE

103. Salad greens will keep dry and crisp much longer when washed, dried, and stored in your salad spinner in the refrigerator.

—MARIE SIMMONS

OR

104. Wash and dry salad greens or sandy herbs (parsley, cilantro) in a salad spinner. Roll them gently in paper towels, then dampen the towels lightly, seal them in plastic bags, and store in the refrigerator. *Greens will stay fresh this way five to seven days; herbs two to three weeks.* Store arugula and basil the same way, but do not wash until you're ready to use them. As a rule, thyme, rosemary, and sage need no washing.

—SALLY SCHNEIDER

OR

105. If you're going to serve the lettuce fairly soon, just tuck the washed and spun-dried leaves loosely into the mixing-serving bowl and let the natural drying of the refrigerator finish the crisping.

—SHIRLEY SARVIS

106. Store soft cookies and dry, crisp cookies separately. If you mix the two, the soft cookies will soften the crisp ones.

—ROSE LEVY BERANBAUM, adapted from *Rose's Christmas Cookies* (William Morrow)

107. To "hold" hard meringues made in advance, place them in a cardboard box and wrap snugly with plastic wrap.

—MARCEL DESAULNIERS

108. Most cooks automatically label foods prepared specifically for freezing. But don't forget to slap a label on those leftovers you hastily shove in the freezer— you may not recognize them next month.

—ELIZABETH ALSTON

109. Use inexpensive jars with snap-on lids rather than your expensive china to store small amounts of leftovers in the fridge.

—ALICE MEDRICH

110. To keep the sparkle in champagne, stick a metal spoon handle in the bottle, letting the bowl of the spoon rest on top, and store in the refrigerator. This works for a day or two only.

—TINA UJLAKI

111. To keep plastic food wrap from sticking to itself, store in the freezer or refrigerator.

—*Conventional kitchen wisdom*

112. When storing a delicate china tea or coffee pot, protect the spout by slipping the cardboard roller from toilet paper over it.

—FRIEDA ARKIN, adapted from *The Complete Book of Kitchen Wisdom* (Henry Holt)

Pinching Pennies

113. Take full advantage of meat sales. Buy a quantity of chicken breasts or turkey cutlets, for instance. Pound them quickly on sheets of wax paper, then stack, seal in plastic bags, and place in the freezer. No need to thaw before using—simply cook in a little olive oil or butter over high heat, deglaze the pan with wine or brandy, and stir in mustard or sour cream seasoned with chopped olives or anchovies.

—Jim Fobel

114. When you cook a whole chicken, take the carcass and any leftover bits and place them in a self-sealing plastic bag in the freezer. Parsley stems, carrot peel, onion scraps, even shrimp shells, and beef bones can be similarly collected and frozen. When you need a stock or soup base, simply dump the contents of one or two bags in a pot, cover with water, and simmer.

—Priscilla Martel

OR

115. Collect tomato seeds, onion skins, vegetable scraps, chicken necks and giblets, and meat trimmings in self-sealing plastic bags and store in the freezer. When you have a bagful, make stock. Freeze it in 1- to 2-cup amounts so you'll always have good stock on hand.

—STEVEN RAICHLEN

116. Learn to cut up chickens, bone meat, and grind hamburger. You'll save a bundle—possibly 50 percent on the cost of precut, prepackaged meat and poultry.

—*Conventional kitchen wisdom*

117. Every time you eat, squeeze, or juice a citrus fruit, use a small knife or vegetable peeler to cut strips of zest. Keep an easy-access jar near the stove to collect lemon, orange, grapefruit, and tangerine zest for flavoring various dishes.

—ROZANNE GOLD

OR

118. Before you throw away a squeezed-out lemon, orange, or grapefruit, remove the zest with a vegetable peeler and freeze. Use lemon zest to flavor salads, stews, soups, muffins, pound cakes, cookies. Try grapefruit zest mixed into the dressing for cooked green beans or asparagus. And drop a long spiral of orange zest into a beef stew. Great!

—CORNELIUS O'DONNELL

119. You can lay a fine grater over your work bowl when making bread or pastry and grate lemon or orange zest directly into the dough. That way you won't lose any of the aromatic oils.

—CAROL FIELD, adapted from
The Italian Baker (HarperCollins)

120. So you don't waste any grated citrus zest, use a mushroom [or pastry] brush to coax every last bit off the grater.

—REGINA SCHRAMBLING

121. Keep bottled lemon or lime juice or strong acidulated water (2 tablespoons lemon juice per 1 quart water) in a spray mister in the refrigerator and spray on cut apples, avocados, peaches, and pears, etc., to prevent browning.

—JA

122. Salvage overripening fruit by turning it into a luscious sherbetlike dessert. Select custard-soft Hachiya persimmons (orange-red and pointed), discard the tips, then wrap tightly in plastic, and freeze solid. Partially defrost in the refrigerator about four hours before serving—it should be the texture of sherbet. If you like, dribble a little liqueur in the cut ends for flavor.

—ELIZABETH SCHNEIDER

123. Don't throw rock-hard dried raisins or currants away. Instead, reconstitute them by covering with cold water, bringing to a boil, then setting off the heat and letting stand for 5 minutes. Drain well before using.

—Conventional kitchen wisdom

Or

124. Let the dried-out raisins or currants macerate until soft in a little fruit juice, wine, or spirits. Use the fruit juice in fruit compotes, cobblers, or other fruit puddings. Save the wine or spirits to flavor desserts.

—Conventional kitchen wisdom

125. Don't toss out fresh ginger peels. Freeze them and use later to flavor chicken stocks for Oriental soups.

—Ken Hom, adapted from
A Guide to Chinese Cooking Video
(Videocraft Classics, NYC)

126. Preserve odds and ends of fresh ginger in rice wine.

—Ken Hom, adapted from
A Guide to Chinese Cooking Video
(Videocraft Classics, NYC)

127. Use the tough outer leaves of artichokes to make broth, adding garlic, parsley, and mint. Use it in making soup or risotto.

—Anna Teresa Callen

128. Do as the Germans do and simmer asparagus peelings into a stock that can be used for cooking the asparagus itself or used as a base for soup.

—HEDY WÜRZ

129. Save the nutrient-rich cooking water from beans to use in soups and stews.

—DARINA ALLEN

130. Don't throw away fresh young beet tops. Stem them, cut into chiffonade (thin strips), and sauté a skilletful in 1 or 2 teaspoons butter or oil over high heat until just wilted. Season with salt and pepper.

—JULIA CHILD, adapted from *Julia Child & More Company* (Knopf)

131. To avoid wasting a whole bunch of celery after using only a couple of stalks, freeze the remainder either chopped or entire. Frozen celery loses its crunch but is perfectly fine for stocks, soups, and stews.

—JAMES PETERSON

132. Whenever you use dried shiitake mushrooms, crack off and save their tough skins. Store these, along with broken bits of other dried mushrooms, in a tightly closed jar in a dark place. When you have enough, whiz to a fine powder in a spice mill or a clean coffee grinder. Store in spice jars to sprinkle on and enrich soups, stews, and sauces.

—ELIZABETH SCHNEIDER

133. Whenever you soak dried mushrooms, sieve the soaking liquid, freeze, and use later to enrich the taste of soups, sauces, and stews.

—*Conventional kitchen wisdom*

134. Salvage aging potatoes by cooking, mashing, and freezing. To reheat, warm them at a medium-low setting in a saucepan with a tablespoon or two of milk or water, stirring to prevent sticking.

—JANET BAILEY, adapted from
Keeping Food Fresh
(HarperCollins)

135. Stir bits of leftover mashed potatoes or winter squash into your baked goods (muffins, quick breads, yeast breads).

—KEN HAEDRICH, adapted from
Ken Haedrich's Country Baking
(Bantam)

136. Never throw away water drained from cooked potatoes. Stored in the refrigerator, it will keep 3 to 4 days and can be used in a variety of ways.

—MARGARET HAPPEL

READ ON . . .

137. Mix potato cooking water into soups and sauces to add nutrition and flavor without overdiluting (the starch in the potato water adds body).

—MARGARET HAPPEL

138. Use potato cooking water as the liquid in making bread—it's a great flavor enhancer.

—MARGARET HAPPEL

139. Use potato cooking water as a "secret ingredient" the next time you make chocolate cake. Just substitute it for the liquid called for.

—MARGARET HAPPEL

140. Don't throw away sprouted onions, shallots, or garlic. Peel and slice them lengthwise and add to oil or butter to be used for sautéing meats and vegetables, or for frying breaded chicken and veal cutlets.

—JIM FOBEL

141. Save the loose skin on onions and garlic to toss into the fire just before grilling meats or vegetables. And throw dry fennel tops on the fire when grilling fish.

—CORNELIUS O'DONNELL

142. When using romaine lettuce in salad, trim off and save the leggy stalks unsuitable for the salad bowl. Wash and chop them for stir-frys or vegetable soup, or use as a garnish for Mexican and Asian dishes.

—ANN CLARK

143. Purify oil for frying with a piece of bread soaked in vinegar (but not balsamic—it's too expensive!). Dropping the bread in when the oil is hot will also tell you if it's hot enough. If it is, the bread will float.

—ANNA TERESA CALLEN

144. Hoard shrimp shells, freeze them, and then simmer and reduce with bottled clam juice, celery, onion skins, and peppercorns for a rich base for jambalaya or fish soup.

—CORNELIUS O'DONNELL

145. Cook shrimp shells in a neutral oil, then use the flavored oil in a hot or cold vinaigrette sauce.

—MADELEINE KAMMAN, adapted
from *Madeleine Cooks, Vol. I*
(Breger Video, Inc.)

146. Keep a big jar of olive oil in the fridge and add olives whenever you have a few left over. The olives are perfect for cocktails and the oil is intensified for cooking. When you pit olives, drop pits in a small glass jar and add vegetable oil to cover. The pits will flavor the oil.

—ROZANNE GOLD

147. The film of honey, syrup, or molasses clinging to bottles can be put to good use. Pour hot water into the bottles, shake hard, then use this sweet liquid in making yeast breads.

—KEN HAEDRICH, adapted from
Ken Haedrich's Country Baking
(Bantam)

148. Before you consign a ketchup bottle or mustard jar to the recycling bin, pour in a little vinegar and shake vigorously. Use the mix in salad dressings.

—JA

149. Keep a special carafe handy for red wines left over from the dinner table. When you've collected enough, use in sauces and salad dressings.

—ZACK HANLE

150. Save all kinds of leftover bread—bagels, baguettes, sandwich loaves, rolls, crackers, biscuits—and buzz to very fine crumbs in the food processor. Freeze in self-sealing plastic bags and use for stuffings and toppings.

—CHARLES PIERCE

151. Recycle the plastic containers you get at the deli or salad bar. They're great for storing leftovers, freezing small portions of homemade stock, or temporarily holding chopped herbs, onions, and peppers you've prepared for cooking.

—REGINA SCHRAMBLING

152. Wash and reuse plastic storage bags. Add a few drops of detergent and a cup of warm water, seal, and massage vigorously until clean. Rinse well, turn inside out, and air-dry.

—JA

153. Save vitamin pill jars and use for storing herbs and spices. It doesn't take long to get a matched set.

—JA

154. Even plastic film cannisters can be pressed into KP duty. Use them to store those odds and ends that so often get lost in drawers—pastry tube decorating tips, aspic cutters, spare cupboard door magnets, kitchen matches, paper clips. Label each plainly with masking tape.

—JA

155. If you bake frequently, buy parchment paper in bulk from bakery supply houses (you'll find them listed in the Yellow Pages). It's cheaper that way.

—JAN WEIMER

Prepping Food

Peeling, Seeding, Coring, Slicing, Chopping, Grating & Grinding

156. Be sure your work surface is the right height to make chopping easy, efficient, and comfortable for you. Your arms should be gently akimbo as you chop. If you're too short, stand on a box. If you're too tall, slide a phone book or two beneath the chopping board.

—BARBARA TROPP

157. To deodorize a chopping board, quickly swab with white vinegar, lemon juice, or detergent; rinse and dry.

—JA

158. To core apples and pears neatly, halve the fruit lengthwise, then scoop out the core with a melon baller.

—DEBORAH MINTCHEFF

159. Never peel an avocado if you can avoid it. It's an awkward, slippery process. Instead, with a sharp paring knife, halve the avocado by cutting from top to bottom, down to the pit. Twist the halves apart and remove the pit. Then slice the flesh *in the shell* crosswise. To dice, cut again lengthwise. Finally, with a shallow oval spoon, scoop the slices or dice out of the shell and gently separate with your fingers.

—NARCISSE CHAMBERLAIN

160. The best guacamole is made from Haas avocados, lime juice (not lemon juice), freshly chopped chilies, and cilantro.

—JANE BUTEL

161. For guacamole that's chunky instead of pastelike, cut the avocado with a table knife and fork.

—CRAIG CLAIBORNE, adapted from *Craig Claiborne's New York Times Video Cookbook* (Warner Home Video)

162. For better texture in banana desserts, scrape off the "fur" with a knife.

—DIONE LUCAS, adapted from *The Dione Lucas Book of French Cooking*, with Marion Gorman (Little, Brown)

163. You can clean strawberries (or mushrooms) without making them soggy by rolling them gently across a damp, clean sponge (rinse the sponge often).

—MARY ANN ESPOSITO

164. When strawberries are less than luscious, cut them horizontally to expose more surface and bring out more juice.

—NANCY SILVERTON, adapted from *Desserts* (HarperCollins)

165. To intensify the flavor of ripe berries, toss them in a small amount of sugar, preferably superfine. Let them stand at room temperature for half an hour to an hour, tossing them from time to time. The sugar draws out the berry juices, forming a light natural syrup and concentrating the flavor.

—RICHARD SAX

166. The fastest way to crush berries for a crisp or cobbler? With a potato masher.

—*Conventional kitchen wisdom*

167. When sieving a purée of fresh or frozen berries for an instant dessert sauce, just tap the sides of the strainer so you don't force the small seeds through along with the purée.

—JACQUES PÉPIN, adapted from *A Fare for the Heart* video (Cleveland Clinic Foundation)

168. When you need both lemon (or orange or lime) juice and zest, grate the zest first, then juice the fruit.

—*Conventional kitchen wisdom*

169. When juicing lemon halves, squeeze them through a dish towel directly into the bowl or pot. This way seeds don't fall into the food and there's no juicer to wash. Also, lemon is a good bleach for towels.

—Carol Cutler

170. The quickest way to zest a lemon, lime, or orange leaving all the bitter white pith behind? Use a vegetable peeler.

—Marie Simmons

And

171. It works best if you draw the peeler over the lemon, lime, or orange in a zigzag pattern.

—Marlene Sorosky

172. Wrap your grater with plastic food wrap when grating citrus zest (or ginger and similar fruits or vegetables). The zest will cling to the wrap when you pull it off.

—Thomas Keller

173. Sprinkle a little sugar over citrus zest or fresh ginger before chopping. The sugar not only dissolves and absorbs the juices but also helps spread the flavor.

—Marion Cunningham

174. When a recipe calls for both sugar and citrus zest, strip off the zest with a vegetable peeler and drop into a food processor fitted with the metal chopping blade. Add ½ cup of the recipe's sugar, then churn until as fine as you like. Add to the recipe along with the remaining sugar.

—JA

175. If a coconut hasn't cracked by itself after being drained and roasted, wrap it in a kitchen towel and whack it on the floor.

—SARA MOULTON

176. To remove grape pips, partially straighten a paper clip, slip the loop end into the stemmed end of the grape and wiggle it to loosen and withdraw the pips.

—PAULA WOLFERT, adapted from
Paula Wolfert's World of Food
(HarperCollins)

177. Raisins will dry more easily if you spread them in a pie tin and freeze until firm (the same technique works for candied fruits).

—JA

178. To pit a mango, stand the fruit on its butt end, then with a sharp knife cut from top to bottom skirting

the big central pit. Score the flesh crisscross fashion, cutting *to but not through* the skin. Partially turn each piece inside out so the skin domes upward, exposing the cubes of flesh.

—JA

179. To peel firm, ripe peaches: Pour boiling water over them to cover and leave for 30 to 45 seconds to loosen the skin. Plunge into an ice-water bath to stop the cooking, and with a paring knife carefully cut the skin and slip it off the peach. As you finish each peach, return it to the ice water. This will activate an enzyme that prevents the fruit from discoloring and deepens its color to a golden blush, especially desirable for such desserts as Peach Melba.

—Flo Braker

180. For an easy way to pit peaches and plums, slice them horizontally all the way around, then twist the halves apart.

—Tina Ujlaki

181. To peel cooked chick peas, submerge them in a bowl of cold water and rub them gently between your fingers. The skins will rise to the top.

—Paula Wolfert, adapted from
Paula Wolfert's World of Food
(HarperCollins)

182. Beets, like peppers, are easier to peel if you roast them first. Slip off the skins and refrigerate the beets to use later in salads.

—SHEILA LUKINS

183. When preparing broccoli for a recipe, trim and cut the stalks into 1-inch pieces and cook them about 2 minutes before you add the florets. If you don't need these bits for the recipe, salt and eat them yourself.

—CHARLES PIERCE

184. When cutting carrot matchsticks, use the large end of the carrot for consistent size and better flavor.

—DIONE LUCAS, adapted from *The Dione Lucas Book of French Cooking*, with Marion Gorman (Little, Brown)

185. To de-silk corn-on-the-cob in a hurry, dampen a crumple of paper toweling and rub round and round over the kernels.

—JA

186. To cut corn off the cob neatly, stand the shucked ear in the central tube of an angel food cake pan, then with a paring knife, cut straight down, sending the kernels into the pan below.

—*Conventional kitchen wisdom*

187. Eggplants will rid themselves of their bitter juices faster if, after sprinkling the slices with salt, you stand

them on end—dish-rack style—in a rectangular wire rack over a shallow pan.

—DARINA ALLEN

188. To mince a garlic clove zip-quick, rub it over the tines of the back side of a fork.

—ALICE WATERS

OR

189. Gently flatten the garlic clove with a knife to loosen the skin. Cut the peeled garlic crosswise into ¼-inch slices, stand the slices on end and smash with the side of a knife.

—STEVEN RAICHLEN

190. Before chopping garlic, sprinkle with a little coarse salt. The salt will dissolve and absorb the juices, which helps to spread the flavor.

—MARION CUNNINGHAM

191. To peel fresh ginger easily and with little waste, scrape the skin off with the edge of a small spoon.

—KATHY CASEY

192. If you freeze fresh ginger, you'll find it easier to grate.

—THOMAS KELLER

193. When chopping such fresh herbs as basil and tarragon, sprinkle the leaves with a few drops of olive oil. This prevents (or at least slows) the darkening of the chopped leaves.

—JAMES PETERSON

194. To prevent parsley from flying all over the place when you chop it, place it in a cup or glass and snip it with kitchen shears.

—CARA DE SILVA

195. Smash lemon grass with the flat or ridged side of a meat mallet to release its fragrance and flavor, then chop it as your recipe directs. [The same technique works for fresh ginger and garlic].

—BARBARA TROPP

196. Instead of cleaning leeks whole, cut them however your recipe suggests, then soak the cut pieces in lightly salted water and drain well.

—SANDRA ROSE GLUCK

197. To core iceberg lettuce, rap the core against the edge of a counter, then pull the core out with your fingers.

—*Conventional kitchen wisdom*

198. To cut thin, julienne-style strips of lettuce, sorrel, basil, or other leafy herbs as if for a chiffonade, tightly roll up three to four large leaves and cut crosswise.

—LINDA ROMANELLI LEAHY

199. To keep mushrooms snowy white, soak 10 minutes in acidulated water (2 tablespoons lemon juice or white vinegar per quart of water), then wipe dry and cook as recipes direct.

—*Conventional kitchen wisdom*

200. To pit olives easily, place on a work surface and roll over them with a rolling pin, then pick out pits.

—Marlene Sorosky

Or

201. Whack them with the flat side of a chef's knife or cleaver, roll them a bit with the blade, then pluck out the pits.

—Peter Kump

202. When peeling onions, pour a small amount of white distilled vinegar on the chopping board to neutralize the fumes and eliminate tears.

—Peter Kump

Or

203. To chop onions without tears, set a lighted candle nearby. The flames burn the sulfuric fumes that make you cry.

—Martha Stewart, adapted
from syndicated TV series
"Martha Stewart Living"

OR

204. Hold a slice of bread between your teeth.

—STEVEN RAICHLEN

205. Need only a smidgen of onion? Peel, then score the top of the onion in a crisscross pattern. Turn the onion on its side and slice thin or thick till you have as much diced onion as you need. Store the balance in a self-sealing plastic sandwich bag in the refrigerator.

—JA

206. Yes, you can processor-chop onions without their turning to mush. Peel, halve, quarter each half (or if large, cut into eighths) and drop into food processor. Pulse quickly, keeping your eye on the texture. Four to five zaps should produce coarsely chopped onions, seven to eight moderately chopped and ten to twelve finely chopped.

—JA

207. When a recipe calls for onions, sweet pepper, and/or celery, processor-chop them together, using short, quick pulses until as coarse or fine as you like.

—JA

208. To peel silverskin onions easily, *tearlessly*, blanch them for about 60 seconds in boiling water. The skins will slip off easily.

—JA

209. Before adding raw chopped onions or shallots to a recipe, twist them in the corner of a towel to remove bitter juices.

> —MADELEINE KAMMAN, adapted
> from TV series "Madeleine
> Cooks," Maryland Public
> Television

210. When cleaning chilies, remember that the seeds and veins are the hottest. Wear thin rubber gloves or, after handling them, immediately scrub fingertips and nails with plenty of soapy water and soak them afterwards in salt water. If you should accidentally rub your eyes while handling chilies, rinse eyes thoroughly with clear water.

> —DIANA KENNEDY, adapted from
> *The Cuisines of Mexico*
> (HarperCollins)

OR

211. Use plastic food wrap or bags to protect your hands when working with chilies (either dried or fresh) in small amounts.

> —ZANNE ZAKROFF

212. To chop and seed a jalapeño, cut a narrow fillet along the length of the pepper from stem to tip. Roll the pepper, cut side down, and cut off another strip. Repeat twice more. You'll have four fillets (to chop or mince) and a core with seeds still attached (to discard).

This is a neater, safer method than digging out pepper seeds with a spoon—the hot juices can spray.

—JANE KIRBY

AND

213. Use the same method as described above for bell peppers.

—STEVEN RAICHLEN

214. Raw bell peppers are easier to digest when skinless. Cut them vertically into sections and peel the sections with a vegetable peeler.

—BEN ETHERIDGE

215. When broiling peppers, first cut them in half and remove seeds, then place them cut side down in a pan, and broil about 7 minutes until charred. Cool and peel. This method shortens cooking time and makes the peppers easier to peel because there are no seeds to deal with.

—SANDRA ROSE GLUCK

216. Roasted peppers will peel zip-quick if you wrap them in a cloth or paper towel or stick them in a paper or plastic bag and let them steam for a few minutes. The skins will rub right off.

—*Conventional kitchen wisdom*

217. An inverted bowl works just as well as a paper bag for steaming a just-roasted pepper before peeling.

—Michael McLaughlin

Or

218. A bowl covered with plastic food wrap.

—Tina Ujlaki

Or

219. Roast red peppers on a broiler pan lined with foil and use the foil to seal around the peppers while they cool. The steam that collects will make the pepper skins slide off easily.

—Nao Hauser

Or

220. Instead of steaming the roasted peppers and rubbing the skins off, try rinsing them under very slowly running water in a colander. You'll lose some juice this way, but the flavor will still be good.

—Jim Fobel

221. To make your own chili powder, toast 4 to 5 dried chilies at a time in a 200° F. oven for 10 minutes. Remove stems and shake out seeds. In a spice grinder or electric blender, grind the chilies into powder, then freeze in a self-sealing plastic bag.

—Betty Fussell

222. If chilies have dried and become brittle, heat them for a few minutes on a warm comal or in a warm cast-iron skillet until pliable.

—DIANA KENNEDY, adapted from
The Cuisines of Mexico
(HarperCollins)

223. To "grind" black peppercorns or other whole spices coarsely, place in a small, sturdy self-sealing plastic bag and whack with a meat pounder, a rolling pin, or the flat side of a large knife or meat cleaver. This keeps the spices from flying all over the place and gives you the coarseness of grind you need. Spice grinders are difficult to control and often grind the spices too fine.

—GEORGIA CHAN DOWNARD

224. Instead of dropping peeled potatoes into water to keep them from browning, wrap them in layers of damp paper towels. This is especially useful for potatoes that are to be roasted or used in dishes where sogginess would be ruinous.

—DARINA ALLEN

225. Prepare potatoes and other vegetables for roasting by tossing them in a large bowl with a couple of teaspoons of oil, coarse salt, and freshly ground black pepper.

—REGINA SCHRAMBLING

226. Leave tomatoes unpeeled except for the most refined dishes. The skin contains fiber and nutrients.

—BROOKE DOJNY

227. The quickest way to peel a tomato and an excellent way to wake up flavor in a winter variety: Spear it with a small paring knife, revolve over a gas flame, and peel.

—DIONE LUCAS, adapted from *The Dione Lucas Book of French Cooking*, with Marion Gorman (Little, Brown)

228. Salad tomatoes will lose less juice if you slice them vertically.

—*Conventional kitchen wisdom*

229. To remove seeds and excess juice from tomatoes, cut the tomato in half around its equator and, holding a half in your hand with cut side down, gently squeeze out the seeds.

—MARIE BIANCO

THEN

230. To crush the juiced, seeded tomato, grate the cut side against the coarse side of a four-sided grater or a flat shredder until you are left with just the skin in your hand.

—PAULA WOLFERT

231. If a recipe calls for canned chopped tomatoes and you have only the whole, snip to pieces right in the can with kitchen shears.

—*Conventional kitchen wisdom*

ALSO

232. When draining whole canned tomatoes, cut them in half in the colander so more juice and seeds will drain off. This means your tomato sauces will thicken faster.

—FAYE LEVY

233. To wash gritty, sandy vegetables like spinach, leeks, and arugula, place the trimmed vegetables in a large bowl of lukewarm water. Add a tablespoon of kosher salt, toss, and let stand 20 to 30 minutes. Then carefully lift the vegetables from the water and place in a colander. There will be sand at the bottom of the bowl but little, if any, on the vegetables. Rinse in the colander to be sure.

—ANNA TERESA CALLEN

234. Soaking vegetables in water depletes nutrients and dilutes flavor, so just wrap them in damp paper towels if you cut them in advance.

—DARINA ALLEN

235. After grinding meat, run a piece of bread through the grinder. When you see the bread coming through,

you'll know you've ground out all the meat. And the bread helps clean the grinder.

—GRAHAM KERR, adapted from
Graham Kerr's Smart Cooking
(Doubleday)

236. The no-fuss, no-muss way to mix meatloaf? Pop all ingredients into an oversize, sturdy, clear plastic bag, press out all air, seal, and knead hard. Empty directly into greased loaf pan, patting firmly into place. The same technique also works for chicken, egg, ham, macaroni, potato, shrimp, and tuna salads—but here you only need to shake everything well to combine.

—JA

237. If you partially freeze pancetta, prosciutto, and bacon, they'll be much easier to chop, dice, or slice tissue thin.

—BEN and KAREN BARKER

238. To prepare chicken, duck, turkey, or goose for cooking: Clean the bird thoroughly inside and out, dry well, and rub liberally with distilled white vinegar—1 to 2 tablespoons for a 4½ pound bird, more for larger fowl. This is a Chinese practice that helps eliminate bacteria.

—EILEEN YIN-FEI LO

239. To scale fish with no mess, start with a sharp-edged soup spoon, grapefruit spoon, or blunt-toothed

serrated grapefruit knife and a heavy-duty plastic bag big enough to hold both your fish and your hand. Line the bag with a layer of newspaper to keep the fish from sliding, and prop up the closed end with a bowl. Slip the fish in head first. With a brushing motion, scrape off the scales toward the head.

—JEANNE LESEM

OR

240. Scale fish under running water to keep the scales from flying all over the kitchen.

—MARK BITTMAN

241. Put salt on your fingers when skinning a fish to help you get a good grip on its tail.

—DARINA ALLEN

OR

242. Do as Julia Child does and grasp the tail with a clean dish towel.

—JA

243. Go easy on salt when cooking saltwater fish. It needs less salt than freshwater species.

—DIONE LUCAS, adapted from *The Dione Lucas Book of French Cooking,* with Marion Gorman (Little, Brown)

244. To keep a cooked fish warm while you make its sauce, smooth wax paper over the fish and hold in a warm oven.

—DARINA ALLEN

245. To devein unshelled, headless shrimp, grasp the vein at the head end with the tip of a paring knife and gently but firmly pull it out.

—MADELEINE KAMMAN, adapted
from *Madeleine Cooks, Vol. I*
(Breger Video, Inc.)

246. Shrimp cooked in the shell will be easier to peel if, before cooking, you snip the shells along the back, removing the vein as you cut.

—DIANA STURGIS

247. To make blue cheese, mozzarella, and other soft cheeses easier to grate, place in the freezer for about 20 minutes.

—GEORGIA CHAN DOWNARD

248. Grate Parmesan cheese only as you need it. Pass it in a bowl to sprinkle on soups, vegetables, beans, and pasta dishes.

—LYNNE ROSSETTO KASPER,
adapted from *The Splendid Table*
(William Morrow)

249. To grate just a little Parmesan cheese, use a lemon zester instead of a cheese grater.

—*Conventional kitchen wisdom*

250. No pastry wheel? You'll find that kitchen shears cut through pizza—stringy cheese and all—more quickly and cleanly than a knife. Besides, they won't scratch or mar your pizza pan.

—JO ANN BRETT

251. To prevent milk from catching and scorching on the bottom of a pan when heated, rinse the pan first with cold water.

—DIONE LUCAS, adapted from *The Dione Lucas Book of French Cooking*, with Marion Gorman (Little, Brown)

252. When using tea bags to make a batch of iced tea concentrate, paperclip or clothespin the tea bag tags to the side of the pan or pitcher so you don't have to fish them out later.

—JA

253. To cut butter into bits, slice an *ice-cold* stick lengthwise into thirds or fourths, then into narrower strips, and then cut crosswise into tiny squares.

—TINA UJLAKI

254. To whip cream successfully in warm weather, pour the cream into a bowl and place it, along with your whisk [or beater], in the freezer for 10 minutes before you begin whipping.

—Nick Malgieri

255. A foolproof way to separate an egg is to stand a small funnel in a measuring cup, then break the egg into the funnel. The white will slither through, but the yolk won't. To remove the yolk, simply tip the funnel into a small bowl.

—*Conventional kitchen wisdom*

256. Learn to recognize properly beaten egg whites: *Foamy* means they're silvery with many large bubbles; *soft peaks* means that the peaks lop over when the beater is withdrawn; *stiff peaks* means that they stand straight up.

—JA

257. When folding beaten egg whites into a heavier mixture, always lighten the heavier mixture first with about a cup of the beaten whites.

—American Egg Board

258. For no-mess deviled eggs, put yolks and all other ingredients for your favorite recipe in a self-sealing plastic bag. Knead the mixture together, then snip off one corner of the bag and pipe it into the egg-white halves.

—American Egg Board

259. To steady deviled eggs on a plate, cut a thin slice off the bottom.

—AMERICAN EGG BOARD

260. To tell if an egg is raw or hard-cooked, lay it on its side on the counter and spin. If the egg wobbles, it's cooked.

—*Conventional kitchen wisdom*

261. Use commercial mayonnaise instead of raw egg to make a mock Caesar dressing that's especially good with mild-flavored fish.

—SARAH BELK

262. Add fresh lemon juice and capers to ordinary mayonnaise for a zesty sauce for grilled fish or poached chicken.

—SARAH BELK

263. To avoid overbeating a meringue for a soufflé, mousse, or other airy dessert, hold back about one-fourth of the sugar called for in the recipe, add to the egg whites, beat until firm and glossy, then fold in at the end.

—AMERICAN EGG BOARD

264. It's easier to fill small ramekins with custard if you first put the custard in a pitcher.

—DARINA ALLEN

265. After oiling a mold for a gelatin dessert, invert the mold on a paper towel to drain off excess oil.

> —MADELEINE KAMMAN, adapted
> from *Madeleine Cooks, Vol. II*
> (Breger Video, Inc.)

266. To simplify stir-frying with lots of ingredients, load prepped, chopped foods on paper plates that can be arranged in convenient cooking order, even stacked to save space.

> —KATHARINE KAGEL

267. Brazil nuts will be easier to crack and shell if you freeze them.

> —*Conventional kitchen wisdom*

268. The easiest way to skin hazelnuts is to roast them first (20 to 25 minutes in a 325° F. oven or until they smell irresistible). While hot, bundle in a clean terry towel and rub briskly. Most of the skins will slake off. Don't worry about recalcitrant bits. They'll add color and flavor.

> —*Conventional kitchen wisdom*

269. To chop soft nuts such as walnuts or pecans, place them in a plastic bag, press out surplus air, and seal. Whack the bag several times with a meat pounder.

> —CAROLE WALTER

270. To crush crackers or cookies quickly and neatly, place in a self-sealing plastic bag, then roll with a rolling pin.

—*Conventional kitchen wisdom*

271. If you want breading to stick, refrigerate the breaded food 20 minutes before cooking.

—*Conventional kitchen wisdom*

272. When dusting a food with seasoned flour, put the flour in a pie plate lined with wax paper so you can lift up the edges of the paper to dust the food without flouring your hands.

—SARA MOULTON

273. Molasses, corn syrups, and other sticky ingredients will slide right out of a measuring cup if you spray it with nonstick cooking spray or oil it well.

—DEBORAH MINTCHEFF

AND

274. . . . off a measuring spoon if you dip it first in hot water.

—DANA JACOBI

275. When transferring chopped, diced, or sliced foods from cutting board to pan or bowl, use the dull—*not the sharp*—edge of your chopping knife. Or use a pancake turner or pastry scoop.

—JO ANN BRETT

276. To keep a cutting board from slipping as you chop, or a bowl from sliding as you mix, dampen a paper towel and place it under the board or bowl before you begin. When you finish, use the towel to clean the counter.

—MICHELE SCICOLONE

AND

277. To anchor a pastry cloth, tape each corner to the counter with masking tape.

—JO ANN BRETT

278. Use scissors to trim the pastry overhang on a pie. It's quicker, easier, and neater than using a knife.

—JO ANN BRETT

COOKING
Across-the-Board Tips

279. To avoid the embarrassment of realizing, halfway through preparing a meal, that you've forgotten to turn on the oven, always turn the oven on *first*. (Especially if turkey is on the menu.)

—ANN CLARK

280. Always start with cold tap water when cooking. It has fewer mineral deposits than hot water.

—*Conventional kitchen wisdom*

281. Don't salt water until it comes to a boil! Salted water has a higher boiling point, so will take longer.

—BROOKE DOJNY

282. Never cook mushrooms in aluminum pans; the mushrooms will darken.

—JACQUES PÉPIN, adapted from *A French Chef Cooks at Home* (Simon & Schuster)

283. Wine corks contain tannin. Drop one into a pot of stew or octopus to tenderize the meat.

—LIDIA BASTIANICH, adapted from
La Cucina di Lidia, with Jay
Jacobs (Doubleday)

284. Use tongs or a flat utensil to turn meat during cooking. A fork will puncture the seared crust, releasing the meat's juices and leaving it dry.

—*Conventional kitchen wisdom*

285. To brown meat for a stew or pot roast in the oven rather than in a skillet, place the rack in the center of the oven, preheat the oven to 500° F., and place meat in a single layer in a large roasting pan. (If the meat is very lean, brush with a little butter or oil.) Roast the meat until nicely browned, then transfer to stew pan. Add a little water to the roasting pan, scrape up the browned bits and add this mixture to the stew.

—BARBARA KAFKA

286. Don't salt meat before you cook it. The salt forces the juices out and impedes browning. Instead, salt meat halfway through cooking, then taste when the meat is done and adjust the salt as needed.

—*Conventional kitchen wisdom*

287. Do as professional chefs do and roast diced onions, carrots, and celery in the pan right along with meat or poultry. With the vegetables cooked down and

flavored with the meat juices, you've the base for a wonderful gravy.

—*Conventional kitchen wisdom*

288. Instead of salting gravy, enrich both color and flavor with a little soy sauce.

—*Conventional kitchen wisdom*

289. To learn how long to cook fish, measure at the thickest point, then allow 10 minutes per inch. This applies to all methods of cooking—broiling, frying, grilling, poaching, steaming.

—*Conventional kitchen wisdom*

290. When poaching fish, let the water return to a simmer before you begin timing the cooking.

—*Conventional kitchen wisdom*

291. Many recipes suggest cooking fish until it flakes. It should *almost* flake; if it actually flakes it's overdone.

—JULIA CHILD, adapted from
"Dishing with Julia," TV Food
Network

292. When shrimp curl into a semicircle they're done. When tightly coiled, they're overdone.

—*Conventional kitchen wisdom*

293. Three signs that it's time to take the custard off the heat: (1) When the foam moves in large bubbles to the edge of the pan, (2) when the custard sauce coats the back of your wooden spatula, (3) when you can make a path through the sauce with the tip of your finger.

> —MADELEINE KAMMAN, adapted
> from *Madeleine Cooks, Vol. II*
> (Breger Video, Inc.)

Pasta, Rice & Grains

294. To give rice a Mediterranean flavor, add a little olive oil and lemon zest to the cooking water.

—Sarah Belk

295. Try cooking a large amount of white rice and wild rice mixed. Divide the mixture into smaller portions and freeze in self-sealing plastic bags. Use it to make mock pilaf with orzo, slivered almonds, and spices—whatever combinations you fancy.

—Jessica Harris

296. Freeze serving-size portions of rice and pasta salads, and pack in lunch boxes still frozen. By lunchtime they will be ready to eat.

—Joanne Hayes

297. If dinner must wait, you can keep cooked rice hot and fluffy by laying a slice of dry bread on top, then clapping on the lid.

—*Conventional kitchen wisdom*

298. Don't wash risotto rice before cooking because you'll lose starches vital to the dish. Instead, toast the rice in olive oil or butter so that each grain is lightly coated. This way, the rice will absorb the cooking liquid gradually and release its starches slowly—necessary for creamy risotto.

—LIDIA BASTIANICH, adapted from
La Cucina di Lidia, with Jay
Jacobs (Doubleday)

299. If you're using wine in a risotto, add it first—before any other liquid—so that the dry rice will quickly absorb its flavor.

—LIDIA BASTIANICH, adapted from
La Cucina di Lidia, with Jay
Jacobs (Doubleday)

300. To prevent polenta from clumping, it is not necessary to filter the cornmeal grains carefully through your fingers into boiling water. Instead, start with cold water, add the polenta in one swoop, turn on the heat, and stir frequently. The polenta won't clump and it will cook faster.

—JOHN MARIANI

301. Always cover your pasta pot after putting the pasta in so it will return quickly to a boil and prevent your pasta from sticking together.

—ANNA TERESA CALLEN

302. When cooking pasta or heating soup, use the pasta plates or soup bowls as lids for the pasta water or

simmering soup. This saves the trouble of heating plates in the oven.

—JAMES PETERSON

303. Always cook pasta in salted water, but don't add the salt until the water boils. You'll need 2 tablespoons of kosher salt for 1 pound of pasta.

—ANNA TERESA CALLEN

304. To cut down on sodium, add a squeeze of lemon juice or a shot of vinegar to the pasta cooking water instead of salt.

—ANNA TERESA CALLEN

305. Never add oil to the pasta cooking water. It will make the sauce slide off the pasta.

—ANNA TERESA CALLEN

306. Never overdrain pasta and be sure to reserve some of the cooking water to loosen it up, if necessary.

—ANNA TERESA CALLEN

307. Use factory-made boxed pasta with sauces that have an olive oil base; fresh homemade pasta with butter- or cream-based sauces.

—MARCELLA HAZAN

308. Cooked dry pasta should be dripping wet when tossed with butter and sauce. And fresh pasta should be very moist.

—JULIA DELLA CROCE, adapted
from *Pasta Classica* (Chronicle)

309. To "hold" pasta made ahead of time, drain, rinse, toss with a little oil, and store at room temperature in a sealed plastic bag or a tightly covered bowl.

—DEBORAH MINTCHEFF

310. If a pasta sauce is olive oil based, toss the pasta with a little extra olive oil before adding the sauce. And if the sauce is butter based, toss the pasta with a bit of butter.

—MARCELLA HAZAN

311. To see how a particular pasta sauce goes with pasta, always taste with a little chunk of bread.

—MARCELLA HAZAN

312. Never serve angel hair pasta with sauce. It is impossible to keep it from overcooking and massing together. In Italy it is served only in broth.

—MARCELLA HAZAN

313. If a pasta sauce is very thick, thin it with a little of the hot cooking water from the pasta before tossing. You'll find that it distributes much more evenly.

—JULIA DELLA CROCE, adapted from *Pasta Classica* (Chronicle)

314. If the tomatoes you're using in a sauce need to cook very briefly, peel them raw with a vegetable peeler instead of blanching so that they maintain their firmness. Tomatoes peeled this way are also sweeter in a salad.

—MARCELLA HAZAN

315. Never add Parmesan to pasta served with a fish or shellfish sauce.

—MARCELLA HAZAN

316. For more flavorful baked pasta dishes, rub your baking pan with butter, then sprinkle with grated lemon or orange zest. The pasta will come out of the oven infused with the welcoming citrus flavor.

—PATRICIA WELLS, adapted from
Patricia Wells' Trattoria (William
Morrow)

317. If you are inexperienced at making your own pasta, wait for a dry day. Humidity makes the dough harder to roll.

—JULIA DELLA CROCE, adapted
from *Pasta Classica* (Chronicle)

318. Don't make pasta near a radiator, fireplace, or hot oven. The dough must be kept soft and pliable if you're to knead, roll, and cut it easily.

—JULIA DELLA CROCE, adapted
from *Pasta Classica* (Chronicle)

319. Color tomato pasta dough with tomato paste rather than the thinner tomato sauce.

—JULIA DELLA CROCE, adapted
from *Pasta Classica* (Chronicle)

BLANCHING/BOILING/ POACHING/STEAMING/ STEWING

320. When boiling a piece of meat (beef tongue, pork, or chicken) tie it round with a string and attach the loose end of the string to the kettle handle. This makes it easy to haul out the meat and check for doneness.

—JULIA CHILD, adapted from *Julia Child & More Company* (Knopf)

321. Poach a whole chicken in an oven roasting bag with the open end cut in half and tied tightly to keep juices in. Place the bagged chicken in a pot of boiling water breast side down and weighted with a heavy lid to keep it submerged. When done, snip one corner of the bag to release juices into a pan; reduce and enrich for a sauce.

—MADELEINE KAMMAN, adapted from *Madeleine Cooks Chicken* (Breger Video, Inc.)

322. Buy chicken breasts with the bone in and lift off the flesh. Place both bones and breasts in a pan of lightly salted cold water together with a quartered onion and diced carrot, bring to a boil, reduce heat, and simmer. By the time the breasts are done, you'll have flavorful stock for a sauce.

—CHARLES PIERCE

323. Try steaming fish steaks wrapped in large romaine leaves.

—MADELEINE KAMMAN, adapted
from TV series "Madeleine
Cooks," Maryland Public TV

324. Stand asparagus spears, points up, in a glass or pyroceram coffeepot, add water, cover, and use the pot as a steamer.

—EMERIL LAGASSE, adapted from
"How To Boil Water," TV Food
Network

OR

325. For perfectly poached asparagus, lay peeled stalks in a large enameled skillet, tips pointing the same way. Pour in enough lightly salted boiling water to cover, put the lid on, and simmer 5 minutes exactly. Drain, return skillet to heat, and shake briefly to rid asparagus of excess moisture. Add butter or sauce and shake a few seconds longer.

—JA

326. Never use a metal pan for cooking or steaming asparagus; the asparagus will discolor the metal.

> —EMERIL LAGASSE, adapted from "How To Boil Water," TV Food Network

327. Never add a pinch of baking soda to the cooking water to brighten snap beans or other green vegetables. It makes them "soapy" and destroys some of their vitamin C.

> —JA

328. The best way to prepare stringy, over-the-hill green beans is to boil them and purée them.

> —SIMONE BECK, adapted from *Food and Friends* (Viking Penguin)

329. To rid dried peas and beans of some of their "gas," use fresh water (instead of their soaking water) to cook them.

> —*Conventional kitchen wisdom*

330. Don't salt dried peas or beans until after they're cooked. The salt not only toughens them but also concentrates as the liquid boils away.

> —*Conventional kitchen wisdom*

331. You'll toughen dried peas or beans if you cook them with acid foods—tomatoes, for example.

Instead, cook the peas or beans until tender, then mix in the tomatoes.

—JA

332. The longer dried peas or beans have been stored, the longer they will take to cook.

—*Conventional kitchen wisdom*

333. To prepare cabbage, lettuce, or other leaves for stuffing, first wilt them in boiling water, then whack the main rib with the blunt side of a knife so the leaves will roll more smoothly.

—Lorenza de'Medici, adapted
from "The de'Medici Kitchen,"
PBS Television

334. Vegetables such as cauliflower, broccoli, and cabbage often take on unpleasant flavors and give off unpleasant odors during cooking. A large piece of stale bread added to the pot as the water begins to boil will counteract both.

—Simone Beck, adapted from
Food and Friends (Viking
Penguin)

335. To brighten and set the color of beets and red cabbage, add a little vinegar to the cooking water.

—*Conventional kitchen wisdom*

336. Never salt the cooking water for corn-on-the-cob. It will toughen the kernels. Add a pinch of sugar, if

you like, to keep the corn sweet and tender. Or cook in a half-and-half mixture of milk and water.

—JA

337. Vegetables like salsify and artichoke turn black when cut or peeled. To help preserve their color, submerge immediately afterwards in about 2 quarts of water acidulated with ½ cup wine vinegar. Cooking these vegetables in acidulated water will also help.

—SIMONE BECK, adapted from
Food and Friends (Viking
Penguin)

338. To keep cauliflower snowy as it cooks, add 2 tablespoons lemon juice or white vinegar to the cooking water.

—*Conventional kitchen wisdom*

339. Onions will boil more quickly and evenly if you make X-shaped cuts in the root ends.

—LINDA and FRED GRIFFITH

340. If you add a little vinegar to the water when boiling peeled potatoes, it causes them to form a light crust that helps them hold their shape when combined with other foods—a special boon when making potato salad.

—EARL PEYROUX

341. A foolproof way to avoid overcooking fragile snowpeas: Put snowpeas in a colander in the sink and

pour boiling water over them until the color is right. Then immediately flood them with cold water to stop the cooking and set the color.

—Lyn Stallworth

342. Don't cook tomatoes at a rolling boil. They'll burst and turn acidic. For sweet, mellow tomatoes, simmer slowly—no additional sugar needed.

—Jack Ubaldi, adapted from *Jack Ubaldi's Meat Book*, with Elizabeth Crossman (Collier, Macmillan)

343. To mellow the flavor of tomato or marinara sauce, add a finely chopped carrot at the outset.

—Michele Urvater

344. To blanch a small amount of vegetables, put them in a long-handled wire sieve and submerge briefly in boiling water, then plunge the sieve of vegetables into ice water, then withdraw and shake well to drain.

—*Conventional kitchen wisdom*

345. When poaching fruit that has a tendency to "brown" for purées, sorbets, or fruit desserts, add vitamin C tablets to the cooking liquid (two 500-milligram tablets per quart of water will keep apples, peaches, and pears bright).

—Ben and Karen Barker

346. Another way to keep fruit from darkening as it poaches is to keep it submerged in the cooking liquid. Cut or punch a hole in a piece of parchment or wax paper, and use it to cover the fruit. Push the paper well beneath the surface of the liquid and the hole will ensure that it stays there.

—NICK MALGIERI

OR

347. Use a heavy plate to weight down poaching fruit and keep it beneath the surface.

—LEAH STEWART

348. You should be able to put your hand comfortably on the side of the saucepan when making hollandaise sauce. If the pan's too hot to touch, it's too hot for the sauce.

—DARINA ALLEN

FRYING/BROILING/ GRILLING

349. Put a drop or two of oil in your skillet and rub it with paper towels to get the benefits of nonstick cooking spray—*without* aerosol.

—TINA UJLAKI

350. To improve the flavor of any cooking fat, add a few tablespoons of bacon drippings.

—JAMES VILLAS

351. Use a pancake turner to flip fragile breaded foods in the skillet. Tongs might shatter the crust.

—*Conventional kitchen wisdom*

352. To tell if oil is hot enough for frying, place the tip of a large wooden or bamboo chopstick at the bottom of the wok or deep-fat fryer. If bubbles rise briskly around the end of the chopstick the instant you insert it, the oil is ready to use. Do the chopstick test several times as the oil gradually comes up to frying temperature.

—Martin Yan

Or

353. If you hear a *whoosh* when you add food to a skillet, it's hot enough to begin cooking.

—*Conventional kitchen wisdom*

354. If food pops up when added to oil for deep-frying, the oil is hot enough to begin cooking.

—Ken Hom, adapted from *A Guide to Chinese Cooking* (Videocraft Classics, NYC)

355. If you see a puff of steam when you add food to a wok [or skillet], the oil is not hot enough.

—Ken Hom, adapted from *A Guide to Chinese Cooking* (Videocraft Classics, NYC)

356. When you fry small pieces of food, shake the pan to keep the ingredients moving and flip them occasionally—all it takes is a quick downward jerk to flip everything over.

—*Conventional kitchen wisdom*

357. For the crispiest-crusted fried chicken ever, roll the chicken in buttermilk, then in self-rising flour

mixed with a little paprika and freshly ground black pepper.

—JA

358. When frying chicken, never allow more than ½ inch of fat in the skillet. Cover the skillet for the first 17 minutes of cooking to help keep the top of the chicken moist.

—JAMES VILLAS

359. Never turn frying chicken more than once, and don't fiddle with the drumsticks—they'll cook properly without being rolled around.

—JAMES VILLAS

360. Nothing in heaven or on earth absorbs chicken grease like a brown paper bag. So use that for draining your fried chicken.

—JAMES VILLAS

361. To keep steaks and chops from curling as they broil, grill, or panbroil, slash the outer layer of fat at 1-inch intervals.

—*Conventional kitchen wisdom*

362. Lighten hamburgers by fluffing or aerating with a fork. Simply mix the ingredients in delicately with a fork, letting plenty of air in.

—DIONE LUCAS, adapted from *The Dione Lucas Book of French Cooking*, with Marion Gorman (Little, Brown)

363. When cooking burgers, handle gently. Don't press them down with a spatula to speed cooking. You'll force out juices and make the burgers dry.

—Conventional kitchen wisdom

364. For browner, crispier-crust meatballs, dredge lightly in flour or stone-ground cornmeal before browning.

—Conventional kitchen wisdom

And

365. To zip up the flavor, add salt, freshly ground black pepper, and perhaps a bit of chili or curry powder to the dredging flour.

—JA

366. Keep a plastic squeeze bottle filled with olive oil at hand to drizzle over food or into a sauté pan.

—Julie Dannenbaum

367. To prevent spattering and burns while sautéing, tilt the pan away from you to pool the oil every time you add more food, then lay the pan flat again.

—Sandra Rose Gluck

368. For extra flavor, fry French fries in top-quality olive oil.

—Martha Stewart, adapted
from syndicated TV series
"Martha Stewart Living"

369. If you want crisply sautéed, golden brown onions, potatoes, zucchini, or other vegetables, heat the
oil first, then add the vegetables but do not salt—salt
impedes browning. On the other hand, if you want the
vegetables soft and moist, heat the oil, vegetables, and
salt together.

> —PATRICIA WELLS, adapted from
> *Patricia Wells' Trattoria* (William
> Morrow)

370. To keep crêpes from sticking to the pan, add a bit
of melted butter to the batter just before using.

> —DARINA ALLEN

371. Don't stir ingredients as you add them to a wok.
You'll cool the wok and make the food greasy.

> —KEN HOM, adapted from *A
> Guide to Chinese Cooking*
> (Videocraft Classics, NYC)

372. To keep bamboo or wooden skewers from burning, soak for several hours in water before using.

> —*Conventional kitchen wisdom*

373. Throw some peppers or onions on the grill to
char while you wait for the coals to turn ashen. They'll
go well with whatever's on the menu.

> —TINA UJLAKI

374. When grilling a tapered piece of meat, fish, or poultry, place the skinny end away from the fire so the food will cook evenly.

—*Conventional kitchen wisdom*

375. When grilling fish on the stove top or outdoor grill, spread the butter on the fish instead of on the grill.

—DARINA ALLEN

376. Thread shrimp onto skewers lengthwise so they won't curl as they grill. They're also less likely to fall into the fire.

—*Conventional kitchen wisdom*

377. A spray mister is great for applying *thin* marinades and bastes to food being broiled or grilled.

—JA

378. Use a spray mister to douse small flare-ups on the outdoor grill or to cool a fire that's too hot.

—DARINA ALLEN

379. To smoke food on the grill, first sear and halfway cook it, then remove from grill, and add damp, non-resinous branches to the fire. Replace food on the grill and cover it with a dome-shaped lid. The dome will capture the smoke and flavor the food.

—MICHEL GUÉRARD, adapted from *Michel Guérard's Cuisine Gourmand* (William Morrow)

380. Vegetables too often come off the outdoor grill charred on the outside and raw in the middle. Try microwaving them first (3 minutes at 100 percent power for sliced zucchini, eggplant, onions), then brush with olive oil, and grill until tender, turning once.

—MARIE BIANCO

381. After you've used a grill and while it's still hot, scrape off food bits with a metal-bristle brush to keep them from hardening and charring next time you cook out.

—MICHEL GUÉRARD, adapted from
*Michel Guérard's Cuisine
Gourmand* (William Morrow)

382. When you broil meat, place the broiler rack over a pan of water. Grease will drop into the water and not stick to the pan, making cleanup easier.

—MARIALISA CALTA

383. To catch grease and discourage broiler fires, put a piece of bread in the bottom of the broiler pan.

—JAMES BEARD, adapted from
Simple Foods (Macmillan)

384. If you want to use your wok as a steamer and your steamer basket is too big to fit inside it, elevate the steamer on an empty tin can or inverted bowl.

—KEN HOM, adapted from *A
Guide to Chinese Cooking*
(Videocraft Classics, NYC)

Baking/Roasting

385. To check meat for doneness without a thermometer, place a metal skewer into the thickest part of the meat and wait 30 seconds. Then remove the skewer and touch it to your bottom lip. If the skewer is cold, the meat is underdone; if skewer is warm, the meat is rare; if skewer is hot, the meat is well done.

> —Patricia Wells, adapted from
> *Patricia Wells' Trattoria* (William
> Morrow)

386. Roll delicate boneless roasts (such as veal sirloin) in crumbs to protect the skin while roasting. Put crumbs on a sheet of wax paper, place the meat on the crumbs, and, holding the edges of the paper with one hand, roll the meat back and forth in the crumbs.

> —Madeleine Kamman, adapted
> from *Madeleine Cooks, Vol. II*
> (Breger Video, Inc.)

387. For a browner, crustier meatloaf, pack into a 9 × 5 × 3-inch loaf pan well coated with nonstick cooking spray, then invert in a shallow roasting pan. Bake as directed.

> —JA

Or

388. Pack meatloaf mixture in a round-bottomed bowl, then invert in a shallow roasting pan and bake as directed, allowing a bit more time, if needed, to cook all the way through.

—JA

389. To give roasts a rich brown finish, rub with flour just before you put them in the oven.

—JA

390. Keep a sandwich-sized plastic bag tucked inside your large can of vegetable shortening. When you need to grease a pan, slip your hand into the bag and scoop up shortening to do the greasing, while keeping hands clean.

—Lucy Wing

391. Simplify cleanup when baking (or cooking) by measuring and assembling dry ingredients on discardable paper plates (the thin, unlined, inexpensive ones). The paper plate becomes a particularly useful tool when baking because you can shape it into a "scoop" and add dry ingredients to the mixing bowl gradually—and *neatly*.

—Gary A. Goldberg

392. To approximate the taste of sourdough, use yogurt in place of milk or water in bread dough.

—JA

86

393. Use nonstick cooking spray to grease the inside of the bowl you'll be using to raise yeast dough, then spritz the top of the dough itself—a much neater method than spreading with oil.

—HELEN WITTY

394. To raise bread dough without guesswork, use straight-sided transparent or translucent containers. On the side of the container, mark the precise height of the dough when you put it in for its first rise. This way you can quickly tell when it doubles (or triples) in volume.

—CAROL FIELD

395. If you're interrupted in the midst of bread-rising, set the dough in the refrigerator. A long, cool rise develops texture and flavor.

—CAROL FIELD, adapted from *The Italian Baker* (HarperCollins)

OR

396. Use the refrigerator method for all yeast bread dough. Place dough in a gallon-size self-sealing plastic bag and let rise overnight in the refrigerator. Next day, shape it in a baking pan, let rise about 30 minutes, and bake. This method gives bread richer flavor and also frees you from waiting for the bread to rise.

—LINDA ROMANELLI LEAHY

397. Wet your hands to keep them from sticking to yeast dough.

—CAROL FIELD

OR

398. Lightly butter or oil or spray your hands with nonstick cooking spray.

—JA

399. If your bread dough seems dry at the end of its last rise, knead it on an oiled rather than a floured board.

—NATHALIE DUPREE, adapted from TV series "Matters of Taste," PBS television

400. For homemade bread that's golden on the sides as well as on top, turn the loaf out and bake on a baking sheet for the final 10 minutes. The pale sides will take on a lovely patina.

—BERNARD CLAYTON, JR.

401. If you make quick breads often, mix up batches of the dry ingredients for your favorite recipes and store them in individual plastic bags, clearly labeled, in your refrigerator. The mix will be ready anytime you are.

—PATRICIA BELL

Or

402. Go one step further by preparing the dry and wet ingredients: Put all the "dries" in one large screw-top jar, all the "wets" in a second jar, then shake each well. Store in the refrigerator until ready to proceed. Shake each jar well again, place the dry ingredients in a large bowl, make a well in the center, pour in the wet and stir just until combined—the batter should be lumpy. Proceed as recipe directs. This works for cookies, muffins, waffles, pancakes, and other simple batters.

—FRIEDA ARKIN, adapted from *The Complete Book of Kitchen Wisdom* (Holt)

403. Don't overhandle dough intended for biscuits or cobbler topping—you'll toughen it. Once the dough is mixed, transfer to a floured sheet of wax paper. Lightly flour the top of the dough, fold the wax paper over it, and gently press to an even thickness of about ¾ inch. Cut as desired.

—RICHARD SAX

404. When making an egg glaze for breads and pastries, beat an egg with 1 teaspoon cold water and a dash of salt, then strain through a fine sieve. This gives you a wonderfully smooth and even glaze. For a really lovely deep sheen, brush your bread or pastry with the glaze, wait 5 minutes, then brush again.

—GEORGIA CHAN DOWNARD

405. To keep muffins from burning around the edges, leave one muffin cup empty, then fill with cold water before baking.

—*Conventional kitchen wisdom*

406. If dinner must wait and the muffins are already done, loosen the muffins and tilt in the muffin pan cups so their bottoms won't get soggy. Set in a very slow (keep-warm) oven.

—*Conventional kitchen wisdom*

407. For muffins, cupcakes, and cookies of uniform size, use an ice cream scoop to apportion the batter or dough.

—JA

408. When filling tins for popovers or Yorkshire pudding, place the preheated tins on the open oven door and pour the batter from a lipped pitcher or measuring cup. This way the tins won't cool down.

—DARINA ALLEN

409. When making biscuits or pastry, to test whether you've cut the butter into the flour completely, shake the bowl. If overly large clumps show up (pea-sized ones are allowable), continue to cut a little longer.

—LEAH STEWART

410. Add a teaspoon of vinegar to pie dough if you plan to roll it right away. Vinegar relaxes the gluten.

—ROSE LEVY BERANBAUM, adapted from *Cookies, Cakes & Pies* (Videocraft Classics, NYC)

411. Always chill pastry dough before rolling and cutting, and always chill it again afterwards, before baking, to further relax the gluten.

—LEAH STEWART

412. Use wax paper to measure pie dough. The standard pie pan is 9 inches in diameter so you'll need a 12-inch circle of dough. Since wax paper comes in a 12-inch width, simply tear off a piece 12 inches long, then roll your circle of dough so it touches the center of all four sides of the square.

—KEN HAEDRICH, adapted from *Ken Haedrich's Country Baking* (Bantam)

413. To roll pie crusts easily and avoid adding excess flour, roll the pastry between two clear plastic produce bags that have been cut down one side and across the bottom and opened—cheaper than plastic food wrap.

—JAN WEIMER

414. When lining a tart mold with pastry, use a small floured ball of the dough to fit the rolled pastry into the mold. No fingerprints, rips, or tears!

—DIONE LUCAS, adapted from *The Dione Lucas Book of French Cooking*, with Marion Gorman (Little, Brown)

415. Freeze a pie or tart shell before baking to minimize shrinkage.

> —CRAIG CLAIBORNE, adapted from
> *Craig Claiborne's New York Times*
> *Video Cookbook* (Warner Home
> Video, Inc.)

416. For perfect pre-baked pie shells, set another pie pan of the same size on top of the pie shell, then turn the two pans upside down and bake for 10 minutes at 400° F. Press down on the top pan to keep the shell from shrinking and bake 10 minutes more. Turn the pans right side up, remove the top pan, and bake the shell 15 minutes longer until golden brown.

> —JIM DODGE, adapted from
> *Baking with Jim Dodge*, with
> Elaine Ratner (Simon &
> Schuster)

417. When beating eggs for chess, custard, or pumpkin pies, brush a little of the egg over the pie shell and set in the freezer for 10 minutes. This helps seal the crust and keep it crisp.

> —*Conventional kitchen wisdom*

418. Baking a pie on a pizza stone absorbs excess moisture and makes the bottom crust crisper, especially if you use a pie tin with a hole in the bottom.

> —ROSE LEVY BERANBAUM, adapted
> from *Cookies, Cakes & Pies*
> (Videocraft Classics, NYC)

419. If you like pies with rich brown crusts, use dark metal pie tins that absorb and hold the heat. Bright shiny ones reflect it.

—Conventional kitchen wisdom

420. Nuts and pie crusts have one thing in common. Both have much more flavor when well browned. Always toast nuts before using them in recipes. And when baking pie shells, ignore the recipe time and bake until deep brown. If the edges threaten to blacken, cover with strips of foil.

*—*JAN WEIMER

421. For a fast and easy tart shell, mix 2 ounces each of butter (½ stick), sugar (¼ cup), and ground blanched almonds (⅓ cup). Mix just enough to hold together and press into an 8-inch cake tin. Bake in a moderate oven until nicely browned. Fill with sliced fresh fruit and pipe whipped cream around the edge.

*—*DARINA ALLEN

422. To line several small tart molds at once, line them up close together. Drape the rolled pastry over a floured rolling pin and unroll across the molds. Use a small floured ball of dough to fit the pastry into the molds, pressing it gently against the contours of each, then roll a dowel or rolling pin across the lot to cut the pastry to size. Remove scraps.

*—*DIONE LUCAS, adapted from *The Dione Lucas Book of French Cooking,* with Marion Gorman (Little, Brown)

423. If you don't have small tart tins, mini-muffin pans work well.

—*Conventional kitchen wisdom*

424. If the crimped edge of your pie is browning too fast, tear off a long strip of foil, fold it lengthwise, and crimp it around the edge.

—Marie Bianco

And

425. If the entire pie is browning too fast, tear off a square of foil, fold in half, then using the fold as the diameter, cut a half-circle. Unfold and lay the circle of foil over the pie.

—Jo Ann Brett

426. To remove the sides of a slip-bottom tart tin, place the tart on a tall can and pull sides downward.

—*Conventional kitchen wisdom*

427. Two sure-fire ways to keep meringue toppings from shrinking. First, spread on the pie while the filling is hot. Second, make sure the meringue touches the crust all around.

—JA

428. Use tapioca rather than cornstarch to thicken high-acid fillings like cherries, which can cause cornstarch to fail.

> —Rose Levy Beranbaum, adapted
> from *Cookies, Cakes & Pies*
> (Videocraft Classics, NYC,
> 1988)

429. Never boil a cornstarch-thickened pie filling longer than 3 minutes. It will thin out.

> —*Conventional kitchen wisdom*

430. No pie funnel? No matter. Make decorative holes in the top crust and insert several pieces of macaroni. These mini "chimneys" allow steam to escape and keep the pie juices from boiling over.

> —*Conventional kitchen wisdom*

431. Before rolling puff pastry, quick-chill your rolling surface with self-sealing bags full of ice.

> —Madeleine Kamman, adapted
> from TV series "Madeleine
> Cooks," Maryland Public
> Television

432. When preparing puff pastry such as Napoleons or patty shells, cut sheets or shells and freeze on cookie sheets or jelly roll pans. When frozen, transfer them to a self-sealing plastic bag and return to the freezer. To use, arrange frozen pastry on a baking sheet and set in a preheated 425° F. oven, reduce heat to 400° F., and bake until golden brown.

> —Madeleine Kamman

95

433. If a cake, cookie, or quick-bread recipe calls for lemon or orange zest, add it to the butter while creaming. Beating releases the flavor of the zest.

—NANCY SILVERTON, adapted from
Desserts (HarperCollins)

434. If while you're creaming butter it becomes runny rather than light and fluffy, shove the bowl in the refrigerator and chill it until firm. Then begin beating again.

—NANCY SILVERTON, adapted from
Desserts (HarperCollins)

435. Always, always line baking pans (cookie sheets, loaf pans, layer cake pans, etc.) with wax paper [or parchment] to prevent sticking (and simplify clean-up).

—IRENE SAX

436. For making delicate cookies (brandy snaps, tuilles, and such) you can't beat reusable, nonstick silicon baking sheets. (Called *Silpat*, they're available from J. B. Prince & Company, 29 West 38th Street, New York, NY 10018; [212] 302-8611.)

—BEN and KAREN BARKER

437. Line the pan for a jelly roll cake so that the parchment or wax paper extends well beyond each end of

the pan. Then when you unmold the cake, you can use the paper overhangs as handles.

—DIONE LUCAS, adapted from *The Dione Lucas Book of French Cooking*, with Marion Gorman (Little, Brown)

438. Foil-line bar-cookie pans (9 × 9 × 2-inch, 8 × 8 × 2-inch, 13 × 9 × 2-inch, and even jelly roll pans). Once bar cookies have cooled, you can lift the foil right out and cut the bars cleanly. The quickest way to line the pans? Turn them upside down and shape the foil smoothly over them, mitering the corners tightly. Lift off the foil "pans" and slip inside the real pans. There's an added bonus: The pans will need only a quick rinse and dry.

—JO ANN BRETT

439. The easiest way to line the bottom of a tube pan? Measure the pan diameter, then cut a square of baking parchment or wax paper of the same dimension. Next, fold the square in half, corner to corner, then in half again and again, until you have a triangle of paper several ply thick. Lay the point of the triangle at the center of the cake pan tube, then mark the outer edge of the tube and also the rim of the pan on the paper. With the paper still folded, cut along each mark. Unfold the paper and you will have an exact-size circle with an exact-size hole in the middle. Use the same technique for cutting layer cake pan liners—omitting, of course, the hole in the middle.

—JA

440. To give chocolate cakes a crisp brown finish, grease the baking pan, then dust with unsweetened cocoa powder, tapping out the excess.

—JA

441. If you like baking, keep two kinds of white flour on hand, one with high gluten content for bread and one with low gluten content for cakes, cookies, and quick breads.

—Beatrice Ojakangas

442. For cakes of exceptionally fine crumb, cakes so light they all but levitate, use single-acting (tartrate) baking powder.

—JA

443. When making an angel food cake or meringues, it's best to use an egg separator to keep the whites 100 percent yolk free.

—Marie Bianco

Or

444. Use three bowls. Separate the eggs over the first bowl, one by one, transferring the whites to the second bowl and the yolks to the third. This way if you break a yolk, you haven't ruined the whole batch of whites. Save all the eggs with broken yolks to scram-

ble or use in recipes where yolks and whites are beaten together.

—NATHALIE DUPREE, adapted from
TV series "Matters of Taste,"
PBS television

445. To use up the yolks, make a custard, chocolate or butterscotch pudding substituting two yolks for each whole egg.

—JA

446. When a butter cake is done, it will shrink from the edges of the pan and be springy to the touch.

—JA

447. As long as a sponge or angel cake "sings" (the soft hiss of the eggs releasing steam), it is not done. When the "singing" stops and the cake is nicely browned and springy to the touch, it's done. Sponge and angel cakes will not shrink from the sides of the pan.

—*Conventional kitchen wisdom*

448. After baking a jelly roll, dust it heavily with confectioners' sugar while still warm and in the pan. Then invert on unsugared wax paper. This is the reverse of the usual technique. And much neater!

—DIONE LUCAS, adapted from *The Dione Lucas Book of French Cooking*, with Marion Gorman (Little, Brown)

449. When frosting cakes, always anchor the bottom layer to the plate or lazy Susan with a dab of frosting. That way, the cake won't slide about as you frost. The technique works for individual pastries, too.

> —ANNE WILLAN, adapted from TV series "Look & Cook," PBS television

450. If your cookies are to bake evenly, your baking sheet must be 2 inches smaller all around than your oven to allow air to circulate.

> —JA

451. When making biscotti or other hand-shaped cookies, dampen your hands with water to keep the dough from sticking to them.

> —MICHELE SCICOLONE

452. To make cookies of uniform size easily, roll dough into cylinders, wrap in plastic and refrigerate from 4 hours to 1 week. Form the cookies just before baking by cutting the dough cylinders into ⅛-inch to ¼-inch-thick slices.

> —FLO BRAKER

OR

453. For drop cookies, use a small ice cream scoop to drop the dough on cookie sheets.

> —JA

454. Because cookie dough is so high in fat, you almost never have to grease cookie sheets.

—Irene Sax

455. If you run out of cookie sheets while baking, spoon the remaining cookie dough on large sheets of buttered aluminum foil. When a cookie sheet becomes free, rinse it with cold water to cool, shake off excess water, and lay the foil with the cookie dough right on the sheet.

—Richard Sax

456. If you must use the lower third of your oven when baking cookies, stack two pans or cookie sheets together to act as a buffer against the high bottom heat.

—Nick Malgieri

457. Double-panning is a good idea whenever you bake cookies because there's little chance of their burning on the bottom thanks to the insulating layer of air. If you use flat cookie sheets rather than the "waffled," put pennies between the two to act as spacers.

—Ken Haedrich, adapted from
Ken Haedrich's Country Baking
(Bantam)

101

458. Cool cookie sheets between batches to keep un-baked cookies from melting and thinning at the edges before they can be set by the heat of the oven.

—ROSE LEVY BERANBAUM, adapted
from *Rose's Christmas Cookies*
(William Morrow)

459. "Pearl" or "rock" sugar has large crystals that add a crunchy texture when used to coat cookies or candied grapefruit peel.

—NANCY SILVERTON, adapted from
Desserts (HarperCollins)

460. In the summer, keep flour in the refrigerator to deter bugs and the effects of high humidity.

—TINA UJLAKI

MICROWAVING

461. If you're nervous about the possibility of harmful chemicals migrating from plastic TV-dinner trays into food as it microwaves, pop the solidly frozen food onto a microwave-safe dinner plate, cover with a large, domed heatproof glass lid, and microwave according to package directions.

—JA

462. To reheat leftover rice in a flash, spread on a serving plate, sprinkle lightly with water or broth, cover with a large, domed heatproof glass lid, and microwave at 100 percent power for 3 to 4 minutes.

—JA

463. Save baked potato skins for a quick hors d'oeuvre, storing in the freezer. When ready to proceed, cut skins into 1½-inch squares; spread on a microwave-safe platter; sprinkle with grated Parmesan, shredded Gruyère, and *herbs de Provence* (a bottled herb mix); and microwave at 100 percent power for 15 to 20 seconds or just until the cheeses melt. Delicious!

—MALACHY DUFFY

464. To cook an artichoke fast, microwave it upside down in a Pyrex® measuring cup with a little water in the bottom (add lemon juice and olive oil if you like). For one artichoke, microwave 7 to 8 minutes at 100 percent power; for four, about twice that long.

—CALIFORNIA ARTICHOKE
ADVISORY BOARD

465. For the best corn-on-the-cob you'll ever eat, lay four large, unhusked ears of corn spoke-style on a double thickness of paper toweling on the microwave oven floor. Microwave, uncovered, at 100 percent power for 10 minutes. Let stand 1 minute, then husk and enjoy (the silks magically come away with the husk).

—JA

466. Microwave unpeeled garlic cloves at 100 percent power 10 to 20 seconds, cool, and store in a self-sealing plastic bag in the coldest part of the refrigerator. Microwaving makes garlic easier to peel and lessens the garlicky smell on your hands. Use the garlic within two weeks.

—DOTTY GRIFFITH

467. To rehydrate sun-dried tomatoes, place in a 1-pint heatproof glass measure with ¾ cup hot water. Cover with plastic food wrap, venting one side, and microwave 50 to 60 minutes at 100 percent power. Stir, re-cover, and microwave at 50 percent power 1 minute. Let stand 5 minutes, drain well, then pat dry on paper toweling.

—ELAINE HANNA

468. For juicier citrus fruits, take from the refrigerator and microwave at 100 percent power, allowing 45 seconds for one fruit, 60 seconds for two, and 1½ to 2 minutes for four.

—JA

469. To dissolve gelatin, combine 1 envelope un-flavored gelatin and ¼ cup cold water in a small heat-proof glass and microwave, uncovered, at 100 percent power for about 45 seconds.

—ELAINE HANNA

470. To melt chocolate, chop fairly fine. Place in a microwave-safe bowl and microwave, uncovered, at 100 percent power, stirring every 10 seconds.

—LORI LONGBOTHAM and MARIE
SIMMONS, adapted from *Better
by Microwave* (Dutton)

471. Use self-sealing plastic bags to melt butter or chocolate in the microwave.

—CAROLE LALLI

472. To soften brown sugar, place in a microwave-proof dish, add a slice of soft white bread or an apple wedge, cover tight and microwave at 100 percent power for 30 seconds. Discard the bread or apple and stir.

—THELMA K. SNYDER

473. To caramelize sugar, combine ½ cup granulated sugar and ½ cup water in a 2-cup heatproof glass measure and microwave, uncovered, at 100 percent power 8 to 10 minutes. Do not stir. Let stand 30 to 60 seconds until the mixture turns a rich amber brown.

—ELAINE HANNA

474. To prepare fresh coconut, drive holes through the eyes, using hammer and nail and making sure the holes go clear through to the open center. Drain "milk" and set aside. Place coconut in a microwave-safe bag and close tight; microwave at 100 percent power for 6½ minutes. Open the bag (beware of steam) and pour any liquid that has collected into "milk" already reserved. The coconut shell will be cracked in several places, making it easy to lift out the flesh. Remove papery brown skin with vegetable peeler and grate flesh in a food processor. An average coconut yields about 2 to 2½ cups.

—BARBARA KAFKA, adapted from
The Microwave Gourmet (William Morrow)

475. Faster and easier than venting plastic food wrap is just to stretch it tight over a dish, then to pierce with a carving fork at 6 and 12 o'clock to release steam build-up.

—ELAINE HANNA

476. Nothing preserves a fruit's natural nutrients, shape and color like micro-poaching. For perfect

poached peaches, combine 2 tablespoons peach or other fruit-flavored liqueur and 1 teaspoon each freshly squeezed lemon juice and vanilla in a flat, microwave-proof 2-quart casserole. Arrange 4 halved and pitted ripe peaches skin-side down in casserole, cover with lid or vented plastic food wrap and microwave at 100 percent power 2 minutes. Turn peaches over, re-cover and cook 1 to 3 minutes at 100 percent power until tender. Let stand 3 minutes, uncovered. Slip the skins off and serve warm or chilled with the casserole juices.

—THELMA K. SNYDER

477. To soften bananas for banana bread and muffins, pierce unpeeled bananas once or twice and microwave, uncovered, at 100 percent power for 1 minute, turning over at half time. Cool and peel.

—ELAINE HANNA

478. "I wouldn't dream of making applesauce except by microwave." For supersonic applesauce for 4 to 6 persons, wash, quarter and core (but do not peel) 2 pounds apples (Macs, Jonathans, Empires, Cortlands or a mix) and microwave at 100 percent power in a covered 3-quart heatproof glass casserole 12 to 14 minutes. Put through a food mill and sprig still-warm applesauce with a cinnamon stick. Or stir in 1 teaspoon vanilla.

—MARIE SIMMONS

OR

479. For gorgeous color, use a 50-50 mix of apples and purple plums, adding ¼ cup sugar to sweeten.

—MARIE SIMMONS

OR

480. For a dessert-rich applesauce, microwave the 2 pounds prepared apples along with 5 tablespoons brandy, 4 tablespoons butter, ¼ cup firmly packed light brown sugar and ¼ teaspoon ground cinnamon.

—MARIE SIMMONS

481. If a baked custard—either savory or sweet—is still soupy after 25 to 30 minutes in the oven, transfer to the microwave, give it 1 minute at 100 percent power, then let stand 1 minute.

—BARBARA DESKINS

482. If you need room-temperature egg whites for a recipe and only have refrigerator-cold, don't panic. You can warm them gently by microwave, 3 whites at a time. Separate the eggs (much easier if eggs are cold), place 3 whites in a bowl and microwave, uncovered, for 30 seconds at 30 percent power. If you need 6 whites, do in two batches, if nine, do in three.

—BEA CIHAK

483. To avoid boil-overs, microwave oatmeal in a 4-cup heatproof glass measure instead of in individual serving bowls.

—MARIE SIMMONS

484. The little plastic squares used to seal bags of bread and rolls make dandy closures for bags used to microwave food.

—ELAINE HANNA

485. Rock-hard winter squash (acorn, butternut, spaghetti, etc.) will be easier—and safer—to cut if you microwave them, uncovered, at 100 percent power for about 2 minutes. Large Hubbard squash may need an additional minute.

—ELAINE HANNA

486. If you store English muffins in the freezer and need to split them in a hurry for breakfast, simply bundle in paper toweling and microwave at 30 percent power, allowing about 45 seconds for one muffin and 60 to 75 seconds for two. They'll soften beautifully and be a cinch to split.

—BEA CIHAK

487. The fastest way to clarify butter? Place 1 stick refrigerator-cold butter in a 2-cup heatproof glass measure. Cover with wax paper and microwave at 100 percent power 1¼ to 1½ minutes until melted. Let

stand, uncovered, 2 to 3 minutes until the solids settle, then gently pour off the golden liquid. Makes ⅓ cup.

—ELAINE HANNA

488. For lowfat berry sauce (great for frozen yogurt or angel cake) in a jiffy, combine 2 cups fresh berries, 2 tablespoons fruit-flavored liqueur, 1 teaspoon lemon juice and ⅛ teaspoon freshly ground black pepper in a 4-cup heatproof glass measure. Microwave uncovered at 100 percent power 4 to 5 minutes, stirring once. Sweeten to taste with sugar. Makes about 2 cups.

—THELMA K. SNYDER

AND

489. For the easiest ever mint sauce, combine 2 tablespoons sugar and 3 tablespoons water in a 2-cup heatproof glass measure. Microwave at 100 percent power 1 to 2 minutes until water boils; stir to dissolve sugar. Add ½ cup finely chopped mint leaves and ½ cup cider vinegar, stir well and microwave 1 minute at 100 percent power. Allow to stand ½ hour to develop flavors. Stored in a tightly covered jar in the refrigerator, this sauce will keep for as long as 2 weeks. Shake well before using. Serve with grilled or roasted lamb, poultry or fish. Makes about 1 cup.

—THELMA K. SNYDER

490. You'll find honey, corn syrup and molasses much easier to measure if you uncap the bottle and liquefy

them by microwaving 30 to 45 seconds at 100 percent power. That's for a 12-ounce bottle. Smaller amounts need even less time.

—Bea Cihak

491. For almost-instant *café au lait*, combine 1½ cups each milk and freshly brewed coffee in a microwave-proof pitcher. Stir in sugar to taste. Microwave at 100 percent power for 1 to 3 minutes or until bubbles begin to form around edge. Whisk until foamy and sprinkle, if you like, with cinnamon.

—Thelma K. Snyder

Or

492. For instant *caffe latte*, combine ¼ cup whole milk and 1 teaspoon sugar in a coffee mug and microwave 45 seconds at 100 percent power. Fill with freshly made espresso (preferably from an espresso machine).

—Marie Simmons

493. Want a jiffy lowfat container for dips and salads that's both crisp and edible? Press an 8- to 10-inch soft tortilla into a 10-ounce heatproof glass bowl, letting the edges ruffle above the rim of the bowl. Microwave, uncovered, at 100 percent power 1½ to 2 minutes, rotating the bowl 180° at halftime, until tortilla is dry and lightly browned. Remove tortilla, dry upside-down and store airtight until ready to use.

—Elaine Hanna

111

494. Soup too thin? Prick a baking potato several times, wrap in paper toweling and microwave 5 minutes at 100 percent power until soft. Peel the potato, then rice straight into soup.

—Cornelius O'Donnell

495. The best way to grill food is the two-step method, that is, to precook by microwave and to finish on the grill. This not only speeds grilling but also ensures succulence. For example, lay chicken pieces skin-side down in a microwave-proof dish. Cover with wax paper and microwave at 100 percent power, allowing 6 minutes per pound and turning and rearranging chicken at halftime. Refrigerate until ready to proceed, then grill chicken 5 minutes on a side.

—Thelma K. Snyder

Make-Aheads/ Freezing

496. Prepare in advance an interesting assortment of canapés: olive or sausage balls, tiny cheese or spinach phyllo triangles, cocktail meatballs. Store in the freezer to pop directly in the oven and quickly bake for parties or unexpected guests.

—James Villas

497. While you're cooking or prepping food, make large batches: lots of fresh croutons, double recipes of salad dressing, triple amounts of chili, spaghetti sauce, lamb stew, and anything else that tastes better the second time around. Freeze surpluses.

—Dolores Custer

AND

498. If you live alone or cook for someone who lives alone, freeze the surplus in small self-sealing plastic

bags. All you have to do when you need a fast meal is pop a bag in the microwave.

—JESSICA HARRIS

499. Cook two briskets at a time, slice, refrigerate, then remove the fat that accumulates. Serve one and freeze the other to serve next time there's unexpected company.

—JOAN NATHAN

500. Make a double recipe of basic poultry stuffing at Thanksgiving, scoop half into a large, heavy-duty, self-sealing plastic bag, spreading as thin as possible, and set directly on the freezing surface of a 0° F. freezer. Come Christmas, all you have to do is thaw the stuffing in the refrigerator; add fresh oysters, chopped pecans, or fruit for variety; then bake as an accompaniment to the holiday bird.

—JEANNE VOLTZ

501. Here's a tip pros use to keep cut-up chicken from drying out in the fridge. This tip will come in handy for your next big party. Wash chicken well, dry, arrange one layer deep on a large tray lined with a towel wrung out in ice water. Cover loosely with wax paper or plastic wrap. Stored this way in the refrigerator, the chicken will remain moist and fresh for as long as 12 hours.

—JACK UBALDI, adapted from *Jack Ubaldi's Meat Book,* with Elizabeth Crossman (Collier, Macmillan)

502. Sauté 6 to 8 boneless, skinless chicken breasts (lightly dredged in flour, paprika, salt, and pepper) in a little olive oil and butter. Add a couple of squeezes of lemon, some grated lemon zest, minced garlic and shallots, a little dry vermouth, and beef consommé. Simmer 10 to 15 minutes, top with lots of capers, and cool. Bundle individually in squares of heavy-duty foil, ladling some of the skillet mixture over each breast, and refrigerate or freeze. Come mealtime, all you have to do is pop the foil bundles in a 325° to 350° F. oven and heat 15 to 20 minutes.

—NATALIE SCHRAM

503. Keep plastic bags of leftover chicken bones and ham trimmings in the freezer and add directly to beans, soups, and broths to intensify flavor. Remove and discard after cooking.

—SALLY SCHNEIDER

504. To prevent freezer burn on poultry bones, giblets, and scraps you're saving for stock, place each batch in a plastic container, cover with water, and freeze. When ready to use, simply run hot water over the container to loosen, then pop the frozen block into a pot with bay leaf, carrot, celery, onion, and more water, if needed.

—ELIZABETH SCHNEIDER

505. Reduced stock can be portioned out and stored in small amounts if you first refrigerate it in a 9 × 13 ×

2-inch pan until it gels, then cut into cubes, transfer to a plastic bag, and freeze.

—Tina Ujlaki

Or

506. Simply freeze the reduced stock in ice-cube trays. When solid, pop out and repack in sturdy self-sealing plastic bags. This is a very convenient, space-efficient way to keep stock for a long time. Use the cubes for soups and sauces, also for cooking grains and vegetables.

—Ben and Karen Barker

Or

507. Freeze your homemade broth in small, self-sealing plastic bags and stack them like tiles in the freezer. Quick to thaw and convenient to handle.

—Beatrice Ojakangas

508. Use ice cube mini-trays to freeze strong mixtures like Tabasco and tomato juice. Nice for Bloody Marys and to add zip to dips and sauces.

—Barbara Fairchild

509. Pesto freezes beautifully. When basil is abundant, make pesto by the gallon and freeze in portions of varying sizes.

—Rita Wolfson

510. Use frozen pesto cubes to add flavor to soups, or defrost a few and top baked potatoes, rice, sliced tomatoes, or pasta.

—CARA DE SILVA

511. Whenever possible, freeze food in thin, flat layers rather than in deep containers. Food will freeze and defrost faster this way, maintaining quality and saving time.

—ELIZABETH ALSTON

ALSO

512. Freeze thin cuts of meat (boneless chicken breast, slices of pork or lamb) rather than big chunks, and freeze them flat and separate. Makes it easier to remove just a few pieces.

—ELIZABETH ALSTON

513. Never try to freeze a whole turkey at home. It's too big, too irregularly shaped, to freeze fast enough to be completely safe.

—*Conventional kitchen wisdom*

514. Soak and simmer the dried beans of your choice until tender, then freeze them in individual containers covered in their own cooking liquid. They defrost quickly, can be used a dozen different ways, and taste great.

—MICHAEL MCLAUGHLIN

515. Prepare long-cooking whole grains, such as brown rice, in the morning while having breakfast. Cover, refrigerate, and then reheat for dinner by steaming in a sieve set over a pan of boiling water.

—KEMP MINIFIE

OR

516. Cook a pound of brown rice all at once, then divide into smaller portions, and freeze in plastic bags or containers for a quick reheat in the microwave.

—CONNIE WELCH

AND

517. Use the frozen rice in meatloaves, in soups, or in stuffing for peppers or cabbage.

—BARBARA DESKINS

OR

518. Keep a pot of cooked converted white rice in the refrigerator to dip into when needed. Serve it as a starch to accompany any sauced meat. Add it to canned chicken broth for a 5-minute soup. Turn it into rice salad by adding chopped bell peppers, tomatoes, and herbs, or, if you prefer, black beans, diced oranges, and chopped cilantro. Use the leftover rice to stretch leftover chili, stew, or soup.

—BEV BENNETT

ALSO

519. When your children complain that their food is too hot or spicy, add a spoonful of rice to their portions to tone down the flavor.

—BEV BENNETT

520. When cooking pasta, prepare enough to last a week. Lightly oiled and refrigerated, it will keep well.

—SANDRA ROSE GLUCK

521. Reheat cold pasta in a vegetable steamer in a few minutes. Or place in a microwave-safe casserole, top with sauce, cover, and heat at 100 percent power 5 to 8 minutes. Stir at half-time.

—JA

522. When freezing eggs, whether just yolks or yolks and whites together, add ⅛ teaspoon salt *or* 1½ teaspoon sugar or corn syrup to every ¼ cup of eggs. Label containers with date, quantity, and type of seasoning.

—AMERICAN EGG BOARD

523. Fresh garlic can be frozen in several forms. You can freeze whole, unpeeled heads and remove cloves as you need them. You can wrap chopped or crushed garlic tightly in plastic wrap and freeze, then grate or break off what you need. Or you can peel whole cloves of garlic and purée them in a blender or mini food processor, using 2 parts oil to 1 part garlic, and freeze.

Finally, fresh peeled garlic cloves can be covered with oil and stored in the freezer.

—GILROY'S FINEST GARLIC

524. When you see irresistibly fresh greens in the market (spinach, kale, collards, turnip greens, etc.), buy a lot, clean them well, and steam until tender. Freeze to use later as a side dish, sautéed, or in soups or pastas.

—TINA UJLAKI

525. If you want to freeze fresh berries individually to use a few at a time, spread them on cookie sheets, not touching, and freeze. Then transfer quickly to self-sealing plastic bags and return to freezer.

—KATHY CASEY

526. Freeze whole lemons or limes. Once thawed, they'll juice like a dream.

—JANET BAILEY, adapted from
Keeping Food Fresh
(HarperCollins)

527. Save prep time by cooking fresh mushrooms ahead of time. Stored properly, they will keep in the refrigerator for two weeks without darkening. First wipe them clean with a damp cloth, then slice whole if small; if large, slice stems and caps separately. For each 2 cups sliced mushrooms, bring juice of 1 lemon, ¼ cup water, 1 tablespoon unsalted butter, and ½ teaspoon salt to boiling in a stainless steel, flameproof glass or

enameled pan (*not aluminum, it'll darken mushrooms*). Add mushrooms to pan, bring to a boil, then boil uncovered 4 to 5 minutes, stirring now and then. Pour all into a ceramic or earthenware bowl, cover tight with plastic wrap, and store in the refrigerator. Use in any recipe calling for mushrooms.

—JACQUES PÉPIN, adapted from *A
French Chef Cooks at Home*
(Simon & Schuster)

OR

528. Save yourself from the tear-jerking ordeal of chopping quantities of onions for holidays or parties by planning ahead. Peel and cut onions in quarters and partially freeze on a baking sheet. Then chop the onions with a sharp knife and refreeze them in a plastic bag until needed.

—JEANNE VOLTZ

529. When sweet red peppers are plentiful and cheap, make extra amounts of red pepper purée to freeze and use year-round. Saves money, time, effort.

—PATRICIA BELL

530. To have fresh serrano, poblano, or jalapeño peppers on hand when you need them, char their skins by roasting the pods over a direct flame. (If you have an

electric stove, broil them as hot as possible.) Let them cool, pop them into freezer bags, and freeze. When thawed, the charred skins will flake off easily.

—BETTY FUSSELL

ALSO

531. Buy sweet red peppers, roast them, slip off and discard the skins, and place the peppers in a container. Drizzle lightly with extra virgin olive oil and sprinkle with freshly ground black pepper. They keep beautifully in the refrigerator for five to seven days and are great for quick weekday lunches, served on toasted whole-grain bread.

—SHEILA LUKINS

532. When washing, tearing, and spin-drying salad greens, it's just as easy to prepare a lot as a little. The greens will keep crisp several days if rolled in absorbent toweling, popped into a self-sealing plastic bag, and stored in the refrigerator.

—BARBARA DESKINS

533. To make salad several hours ahead of time, first make the dressing directly in the bowl. Next cross the serving fork and spoon in the bottom of the bowl and arrange the lettuces on top so they don't fall into the dressing and go limp. Cover the bowl with damp paper

towels and refrigerate until shortly before serving. Bring the salad to room temperature, toss, and serve.

—SARAH BELK

534. Make a large batch of vinaigrette in a mixing bowl, using your favorite mustards, olive oil, vinegar, salt, pepper, and halved garlic cloves mixed with fresh herbs—chervil, rosemary, lemon thyme, whatever. Store it in old wine bottles in the refrigerator where it will keep well indefinitely. Bring to room temperature before serving, and shake well.

—BRYAN MILLER

535. Add 10 juniper berries to a cup of extra virgin olive oil, place in a bottle, and use to add piquancy to pork chops. You can also flavor olive oil with rosemary, thyme, fennel, and other herbs. Store these oils in the coldest part of the refrigerator and use within two weeks.

—ANNA TERESA CALLEN

536. If you have the space, freeze washed whole tomatoes and peppers while they're in season and at their peak of flavor. Peel and chop the tomatoes while still frozen to add to stews and soups. Peppers may also be seeded and chopped while frozen, then sautéed or cooked just like fresh peppers.

—JOANNE LAMB HAYES

537. When home-grown, vine-ripened tomatoes are out of season, roast the supermarket variety to improve and intensify their flavor. Halve the tomatoes, coat with olive oil, place on a baking sheet, sprinkle with salt and pepper, and bake at 150° F. for 8 to 10 hours (or overnight if you have a fail-safe oven) until the tomatoes are shriveled and partly dehydrated but still somewhat moist. Cool, again coat with olive oil, and store in the fridge. These roasted tomatoes will keep as long as three months.

—BEN and KAREN BARKER

538. Slice vegetables in advance for a stir-fry. You can keep them fresh and crisp three to four days by wrapping each prepped vegetable separately in white paper towels, then refrigerating in self-sealing plastic bags.

—EILEEN YIN-FEI LO

539. When entertaining, blanch vegetables in advance, then sauté them just before serving. This makes you less likely to get distracted by conversation and "burn the beans."

—JAN T. HAZARD

540. Rather than chop a small amount of frequently used herbs every time you need them, prepare a lot at once, place in plastic containers or self-sealing plastic bags, and store in freezer.

—FLORENCE LIN

O R

541. When fresh herbs are in rich supply, make ice cubes by inserting whole sprigs or teaspoons of chopped herbs in a tray partially filled with water. When herb cubes are frozen pop them out of the tray and into a plastic bag. Terrific for adding summer flavor to winter soups and stews.

—BARBARA KAFKA

O R

542. Snip fresh parsley, chives, and dill directly from your herb garden or windowsill pots into wide-mouthed plastic freezer containers and freeze to use all winter long.

—MARCIA ADAMS

543. Keep prunes, dried apricots, pears, or peaches in preserving jars and cover with any spirit you fancy: brandy, bourbon, Grand Marnier, Madeira. Then turn them into a quick dessert or use them to enliven breads, cakes, sauces, meats, and poultry.

—JAMES BEARD, adapted from
Simple Foods (Macmillan)

544. You can produce "no-think" muffins and quick breads even before you've had your first cup of coffee if you measure dry and liquid ingredients (kept separate, of course) the night before. Then all you have to

do is combine everything and pour the batter into a pregreased pan to bake.

—JIM FOBEL

545. Crêpes may be "held" in various ways for various lengths of time. For future use, freeze them in layers separated by wax paper. For same-day use, refrigerate without paper linings. For immediate use, keep warm on a plate placed over a saucepan of simmering water.

—DARINA ALLEN

546. Prepare several loaves of yeast bread, shape, and freeze. The day you want to serve the bread, defrost the dough, let it rise, then bake it.

—JOAN NATHAN

547. Always make crêpe, waffle, and pancake batters well ahead of time. They need to stand several hours in the refrigerator before they're cooked.

—*Conventional kitchen wisdom*

548. Enjoy fresh-tasting French or Italian bread every day (without having to shop for it daily) by keeping some in the freezer. Cut into portion-size pieces (4 to 5 per baguette), wrap individually in plastic, and put all in a second plastic bag to freeze. To serve, thaw briefly and heat in a 425° F. oven until brown and crisp.

—SHIRLEY SARVIS

549. When double-wrapped in plastic, unsliced white bread freezes well and when thawed, tastes just like fresh bread.

—RITA WOLFSON

550. Slice homemade bread *before* freezing (in a self-sealing plastic bag) so you can take out only as many slices as you wish.

—BEATRICE OJAKANGAS

551. For quick, delicious croutons: Brush both sides of ¼-inch-thick slices French bread with olive or vegetable oil, quarter each slice into 4 squares, place on a baking sheet, and brown in a 375° F. oven. Cool and rub squares with peeled garlic cloves. Toss into salads, scatter over soup, or seal in freezer containers and store in freezer.

—JACQUES PÉPIN, adapted from *A French Chef Cooks at Home* (Simon & Schuster)

552. Using a stale loaf of non-sour French bread, buzz to crumbs in a food processor. Store in plastic freezer containers in the freezer. Then when a recipe calls for bread crumbs, scoop out what you need and thaw.

—SHIRLEY SARVIS

553. Streusel and crumb mixtures to scatter over fruit desserts and pies can be made ahead and refrigerated or frozen.

—RICHARD SAX

554. Make pizza dough in double batches and freeze half. You can even roll out the extra dough, fit it into a pizza pan, and freeze it flat for a headstart on a fast meal.

—KEMP MINIFIE

555. Freeze pie dough in one-crust wads or discs, tightly wrapped in self-sealing plastic bags you have labeled and dated.

—RICHARD SAX

OR

556. When fruit is in season, make lots of pie shells and fill them with fruit. Freeze the unbaked pies, then bake them in winter (good insurance against drop-in guests). If you and a friend work together, it's both easy and fun.

—JOAN NATHAN

557. Also keep your favorite crumb and nut crust mixtures on "ice," placing in each self-sealing plastic bag or freezer container the amount needed for one pie shell. Once thawed, the crumbs can be fitted into pie pans and filled as recipes direct.

—JA

558. When preparing lunches for your children to take to school or summer day camp, try "drinkable" ice packs: Fill a 12-ounce plastic bottle about halfway

with drinking water and freeze it overnight, tilting the bottle so the water will freeze at an angle (if you freeze it straight up, the expanded water will make the bottle bulge). Next morning pack the lunch, add more drinking water to the bottle, and stick it in the lunch box to keep the food cool and be melted enough to drink by lunchtime.

—MICHELE URVATER

559. Baking cookies is a snap if the dough's already prepared. But different kinds of cookies require different treatment. Here's what baking pro **Flo Braker** recommends:

For drop cookies: Use an ice cream scoop to pick up about 2 tablespoons of dough and place scooped portions close together on a baking tray. Cover with plastic wrap and refrigerate for up to two days. To bake, transfer cookies to a parchment-lined baking sheet, spacing 1 to 2 inches apart.

For hand-shaped cookies: Refrigerate dough in a covered bowl, then shape and bake a day or two later. Or shape the cookies right away on foil-lined baking sheets and freeze, securely wrapped, for up to a week.

For cut-out cookies: Roll the dough into ⅛-inch-thick circles between two sheets of wax paper, then stack the papers of dough on a baking sheet, and refrigerate (they'll hold for a week). Or wrap securely and freeze for up to 10 days. When ready to cut, remove one dough circle at a time, peel off the top sheet of wax paper, replace it loosely with a fresh one, then flip the entire package over. Peel off and discard the second sheet of wax paper and cut into shapes as desired.

Time-Savers

560. Trim kitchen time by buying precut poultry and meats, washed spinach, shredded or grated cheese, presliced mushrooms, filleted fish, bakery croissants, bottled mayonnaises, and condiments. You can produce great recipes by skillfully teaming fresh foods with canned, frozen, or bottled.

—Jacques Pépin, adapted from
The Short-Cut Cook (William
Morrow)

561. Copy your favorite recipes from various sources and keep them in a single binder or file. That way you needn't clutter up your kitchen with cookbooks or waste time searching through bookshelves.

—Dolores Custer

562. For a strenuous but satisfying way to entertain friends and repay obligations, have consecutive dinner parties on Saturday and Sunday evenings. Advantages? You can serve the same menu on both occasions, use the same flowers, and clean the house only once.

—Jan T. Hazard

563. To get a meal on the table fast—either a party dinner or a family supper—put on some zippy music. A march by John Philip Sousa, the stirring circus-parade music "Entrance of the Gladiators" by Julius Fucik, or Offenbach's *Gaitée Parisienne* should get you moving.

—CORNELIUS O'DONNELL

564. For a quick meal, make a one-pot pasta by tossing chopped peppers, zucchini, scallions, frozen peas, or any vegetable you like into the pot with the boiling pasta. Time it so the veggies and pasta are done at the same time, and add bits of leftover meat at the last minute if you have any. Toss with olive oil, freshly ground pepper, fresh herbs, and roasted garlic purée or a little chicken stock, and top with freshly grated Parmesan.

—CORNELIUS O'DONNELL

565. For quick and easy ravioli, fill wonton wrappers with sautéed crabmeat, herbed goat cheese, or any filling you fancy. Moisten edges with egg wash to seal and poach in boiling water.

—LEAH STEWART

566. Sauté vegetables in the same skillet you've used to sauté the meat—no need to dirty an extra pan.

—JACQUES PÉPIN, adapted from
The Short-Cut Cook (William
Morrow)

567. Cook whenever possible in a well-seasoned cast iron pan, which requires no washing, only wiping clean.

—REGINA SCHRAMBLING

568. Try to put foods in containers that can go directly from freezer to oven to table.

—JACQUES PÉPIN, adapted from *The Short-Cut Cook* (William Morrow)

569. To simplify making several recipes at once, prepare the ingredients they have in common (e.g., chopped onions, peppers, or parsley) at the same time.

—SARA MOULTON

570. Save confusion as well as time by cleaning up and putting away, as you work, those kitchen utensils and ingredients you're finished with. An uncluttered work area lets you proceed more efficiently and cuts down on mistakes.

—FLORENCE LIN

571. If you post the family dinner menus, older children can help by putting on the roast or chopping the vegetables if they get home before you do.

—JAN T. HAZARD

572. Keep at least one emergency meal in the cupboard [or freezer]—for example, linguine and clam sauce or sun-dried tomato pesto.

—DOLORES CUSTER

573. When making meatloaf, use bottled marinara sauce instead of canned tomatoes—the herbs and spices are built right in so everything goes together faster.

—JA

574. For a zip-quick meatloaf, pat the mix in a pie pan sprayed with nonstick cooking spray, score in six or eight wedges. A meat "pie" will bake twice as fast as a meat "loaf."

—JA

575. For almost "instant" meatloaf, pat the mixture into muffin pans and brush with pasta, barbecue, or soy sauce. These mini-meatloaves will be ready to eat in 20 to 25 minutes.

—JA

576. It saves time to use a dry roux when cooking Cajun or Creole food. If you start with uncooked flour, it will take 10 minutes or more to turn the color you want; if you have the dark, browned flour on hand, you can save a step by adding it directly to the fat in the recipe. Store it in a tightly capped jar at room temperature or in the fridge.

—EARL PEYROUX

577. Put self-sealing plastic bags filled with ice directly into broth or soup to cool it quickly.

—ELIZABETH TERRY

578. If you want to remove fat from soup or stew but can't wait for it to chill and congeal, draw a slice of bread across the surface of the liquid to soak up as much grease as possible.

—Lee Fowler

579. To cool cut-up onions, peppers, potatoes, etc., for chilled salads in a hurry, spread on a jelly roll pan and set in the freezer. This technique works for all foods that must be chilled fast.

—Sara Moulton

580. To save time, nutrients, *and* color, choose un-waxed cucumbers and slice them with their skins on.

—Lee Fowler

581. Begin heating pasta cooking water when you begin making the sauce. That way it's ready the instant you need it.

—Jacques Pépin, adapted from
The Short-Cut Cook (William Morrow)

582. Instead of blanching cabbage leaves to wilt them for stuffing, simply leave the whole head in the freezer overnight.

—Florence Fabricant

583. To slice mushrooms zip-quick, use an egg slicer.

—JA

584. Buy new red potatoes or California whites and you won't need to peel them before boiling.

—LEE FOWLER

585. Instead of taking time to chop herbs, slip them into the food processor with other ingredients or snip them with scissors directly into whatever you're making.

—GAEL GREENE

586. To ripen a tomato fast, put it with an apple in a perforated bag or a covered bowl. The apple gives off ethylene gas that speeds the ripening process.

—*Conventional kitchen wisdom*

587. Don't bother chopping canned tomatoes ahead of time to add to a long-cooking stew or soup. Just dump them in straight from the can and gently break them up with the edge of a wooden spoon. Give your stew a stir or two to see if you've left any pieces too large.

—MICHELE URVATER

588. If you grow your own lettuces, take a salad spinner half filled with water into your garden and as you pick the leaves drop them right into the spinner. They'll be partially clean by the time you get them to the sink.

—MARK BITTMAN

589. Make a vinaigrette dressing quickly and simply in a shaker jar: Add crushed garlic, vinegar, oil; close; and shake well. Let stand, then shake well again. Use less than you're tempted to use.

—GAEL GREENE

590. Need crushed potato or tortilla chips for topping or breading? Crush them right in the bag. The same holds for stack-wrapped saltines. Give them a couple of good whacks with a rolling pin. Or just squeeze and massage the bags with your hands.

—JA

591. To crush nuts quickly and easily without muss or fuss, place in a self-sealing plastic bag and roll with a rolling pin.

—*Conventional kitchen wisdom*

592. Store honey in a plastic squeeze bottle. This makes it easier to measure in small amounts.

—PATRICIA BELL

593. To separate a lot of eggs at once, break them carefully into a big bowl and then (with your impeccably clean hands) simply scoop out the yolks.

—WHITNEY CLAY

594. Weigh ingredients instead of using measuring cups. This saves steps and dirty dishes and is espe-

cially useful for flour and nuts. Keep a list of equivalents posted for ingredients you use frequently. For example:

1 cup all-purpose flour	=	5 oz. unsifted, 4½ oz. sifted
1 cup cake flour	=	4 oz. unsifted, 3½ oz. sifted
1 cup almonds	=	5⅓ oz. whole, 4 oz. finely chopped

—ALICE MEDRICH

595. Make everything in big batches—soups, stews, even salads. Leftovers go into the freezer or become tomorrow's lunch. A lamb stew, thinned out and blended in a food processor, might have a second life as a sauce for ribbon noodles.

—PRISCILLA MARTEL

596. Whether you weigh or measure ingredients, it's a good idea to attach to your refrigerator or cupboard door your own, individualized measurement conversion chart to remind you of equivalents you tend to forget. This will spare you the trouble of searching through cookbooks when you are doubling or halving recipes.

—JAMES VILLAS

597. When a recipe calls for sifting, it works just as well to put all dry ingredients in the mixing bowl and stir with a whisk.

—BEN ETHERIDGE

598. If grandma told you always to proof yeast—dissolve it in liquid to see if it bubbles—forget it. Today's dry yeast is reliable enough to stir directly in with other dry ingredients, including flour.

—Bernard Clayton, Jr.

599. No time to roll and cut biscuits? Just drop the dough from a tablespoon or small ice cream scoop onto lightly greased baking sheets.

—JA

600. To break up bar chocolate quickly with no mess, leave the wrapper on. Jab through the paper several times with an ice pick, then unwrap, and dump the coarsely chopped contents into a bowl.

—Carole Walter

601. To avoid dirtying an extra pot and possibly wasting some chocolate, melt chocolate in the microwave in the same bowl you'll use to mix in other ingredients.

—Patricia Bell

602. If your oven has a pilot light, you can melt chocolate safely and effortlessly: Just put it in an uncovered bowl and leave it on the oven top several hours or overnight. (Don't try this in a low oven—even "low" will be too hot for the chocolate. And don't try it with white chocolate, which must be stirred to prevent "seeding.")

—Rose Levy Beranbaum

603. When you want to finish freezing ice cream in a hurry, take it soft-frozen from the ice cream machine, spread it thin in a jelly roll pan, and pop it into the freezer. It will harden in about an hour.

—SARA MOULTON

ALSO

604. For smoothly served desserts, scoop ice cream or sorbet ahead of time, place balls in single layers in containers lined with wax paper, and cover with plastic wrap. Kept in freezer, they'll lift out easily when you want them.

—LUCY WING

605. Keep commercially frozen raspberries, strawberries, and blackberries in your freezer to produce fruit *coulis* at a moment's notice. Just thaw, purée, strain, and flavor to taste with a little lemon juice and honey.

—SALLY SCHNEIDER

606. When you make a pie, make a double or triple batch of dough (it's the same amount of work) and freeze it in portions to thaw and roll for a quick dessert. Simplest is to roll it into a big flat circle, cut it into strips or shapes, and bake it like that. Then arrange the crisp crusts over individual bowls of berries or cooked fruit and ice cream.

—SALLY SCHNEIDER

607. Brew after-dinner coffee *before* guests arrive for dinner and keep hot in an attractive Thermos®. You can even set up the complete coffee tray ahead of time, with cups, saucers, sugar, and the Thermos of coffee—plus, perhaps, a second Thermos of hot water for tea.

—PRISCILLA MARTEL

608. Use bottled clam juice as a quick substitute for fish broth.

—*Conventional kitchen wisdom*

609. Instead of buying wax paper in a roll, buy it in sheets from a professional supplier. Then whenever you need a sheet fast, you can yank it out with one hand.

—LEAH STEWART

610. Put telephone and TV time to good use by cutting parchment liners for commonly used baking pans. File the liners by type in manila envelopes, label, and stash in a kitchen drawer for easy access.

—JAN WEIMER

611. Mark frequently used cookbook recipes with paper clips so you don't waste time trying to find them.

—JOAN NATHAN

612. Running out of staples is an especially frustrating time-waster. Put necessities (coffee filters, cat food) on the list long before supplies run low.

—ELIZABETH ALSTON

CUTTING FAT & CALORIES

613. If you use a nonstick frying pan, you'll need only 1 tablespoon of olive oil to sauté vegetables. For a dividend, use flavorful oils—extra virgin olive oil or sesame oil.

—STEVEN RAICHLEN

614. For a low-fat method of cooking boneless chicken breasts, rub them with chopped cilantro and a splash of lime and place in a lightly oiled oven-roasting bag. (To spread the oil evenly, put a teaspoon of corn oil in the bag and massage the bag between your palms.) Cut and tie the open end of the bag to keep juices in and poach in a covered sauté pan.

—MADELEINE KAMMAN, adapted
from *Madeleine Cooks Chicken*
(Breger Video, Inc., 1989)

615. Bake bacon instead of broiling or frying it—more yield, less fat, less curl.

—JAMES BEARD, adapted from "The
James Beard Show," "Cooking
Classics," TV Food Network

616. The easiest way to defat canned broth? Refrigerate the can, open the entire end, and lift off the fat.

—Arthur Schwartz, adapted
from *Soup Suppers*
(HarperCollins)

617. To defat homemade broths quickly, fill a small self-sealing plastic bag with ice cubes and draw back and forth across the surface. The fat will cling to the bag.

—JA

Or

618. Pour the broth through a large funnel filled with ice cubes.

—Paul Prudhomme

619. If you need to degrease a sauce or rich casserole as soon as it has finished cooking, move the pan or casserole partially off the heat; the fat will make its way to the cooler side and rise to the surface, where it can be removed with a spoon. After this initial degreasing, remove the pan completely from the heat and spoon off remaining fat as it rises to the top. Remove any remaining particles by drawing narrow strips of paper toweling quickly across the surface.

—Louisette Bertholle, adapted
from *French Cuisine for All*
(Doubleday)

142

620. After making vegetable juice in a juicer, use the pulpy vegetable residue to make a wonderful low-fat broth.

—Patricia Bell

621. For a lower-fat meatloaf, use very lean ground round and substitute nonfat frozen egg product for eggs (¼ cup = 1 egg). Also use 1½ times the onion and sweet pepper called for and chop them very fine (this increases the juiciness of the meatloaf). To enrich the flavor, mix in ¼ cup freshly grated Parmesan cheese.

—JA

622. Use a small ice cream scoop to measure out and transfer portions of a low-fat meatball mixture from mixing bowl to baking sheet. Bake at 375° F. for 20 minutes or until cooked through. The scoop method saves messy hands and baking eliminates the fat you'd need for frying.

—Jean Hewitt Blair

623. To trim the fat and calories in chili, use ground turkey breast instead of hamburger. Then pump up the beef flavor to taste with beef bouillon cubes.

—JA

624. When browning meat for a stew, use the broiler instead of the skillet. Not only do you use no fat, much of the fat in the meat melts and drips away.

—JA

625. Use low-fat buttermilk instead of beaten egg when breading chicken, and for extra flavor, add a crushed clove of garlic. A good crumb mix: 3 cups fairly fine soft white bread crumbs tossed with ¼ cup each freshly grated Parmesan and minced parsley, 1 tablespoon paprika, 1 teaspoon crumbled leaf marjoram, ½ teaspoon crumbled leaf thyme, 1 teaspoon salt, and ½ teaspoon freshly ground black pepper. Roll skinned chicken parts in buttermilk, then crumb mixture, then bake in a 350° F. oven until richly browned instead of frying.

—JA

626. When making old-fashioned baked beans or such French classics as *Coq au Vin*, use lean smoked ham instead of fatty salt pork.

—JA

AND

627. A few snippets of prosciutto or Westphalian ham can substitute nicely for bacon in quiche. You can further reduce fat, cholesterol, and calories by using nonfat frozen egg product in place of whole eggs (¼ cup egg product = 1 egg).

—JA

628. To reduce calories in your favorite French toast recipe, don't fry it. Bake it instead in a preheated 500° F.

oven on a greased baking sheet for 6 minutes, turn and bake 3 to 4 minutes longer.

—AMERICAN EGG BOARD

629. Make your own fat-free chips by buying good-quality corn tortillas and drying them in your oven.

—TINA UJLAKI

630. Thicken a soup without using flour and butter or eggs—just purée a portion of the soup and stir it back into the pot.

—JACQUES PÉPIN, adapted from "A Fare for the Heart" video (Cleveland Clinic Foundation)

631. Use nonfat sour cream instead of milk or cream to enrich sauces and soups.

—STEVEN RAICHLEN

632. If you don't like the taste of the new low-fat (or nonfat) mayonnaises, you can still reduce the fat in mayonnaise. Simply mix half-and-half with low-fat (or nonfat) yogurt.

—LEE FOWLER

633. Try zucchini "pasta" for a low-calorie change. Cut zucchini into fettuccinelike strips and steam quickly until limp. Top with a tomato sauce and a light sprinkling of freshly grated Parmesan.

—JA

634. Sprinkle balsamic vinegar on baked new potatoes in place of butter or sour cream, or drizzle over stir-fried vegetables.

—LYNNE ROSSETTO KASPER,
adapted from *The Splendid Table*
(William Morrow)

635. Beat hot potato cooking water into mashed potatoes to make them light and fluffy. No need for lashings of high-calorie hot milk and high-fat melted butter.

—MARGARET HAPPEL

OR

636. Whip them up with lowfat buttermilk or yogurt.

—JA

637. Instead of cream, use chicken or vegetable stock in potatoes au gratin and similar casseroles.

—STEVEN RAICHLEN

638. Use nonstick vegetable spray for a quick, efficient, and low-fat way to lightly coat pita triangles, tortilla chips, and phyllo sheets.

—BETTY ROSBOTTOM

639. Instead of slathering butter or margarine on corn-on-the-cob, spray with butter-flavored nonstick cooking spray and be generous with the freshly ground

black pepper. Or squeeze fresh lime juice over the ears and sprinkle lightly with chili powder (or freshly ground black pepper).

—JA

640. Instead of browning sliced eggplant in a skillet (it soaks up fat like a sponge), brush lightly with olive oil and brown in the broiler or on the grill. (To trim the fat to zilch, spray lightly with olive-oil–flavored nonstick cooking spray instead of brushing with oil).

—JA

641. If you cook eggplant whole in the microwave, it requires no added oil and is great for making dips and sauces. Simply prick the eggplant all over, place on a plate, and microwave at 100 percent power for 10 minutes, turning it over twice, until soft.

—CONNIE WELCH

642. Substitute yogurt cheese for sour cream in dishes both sweet and savory. Here's a clean and easy way to make it: Spoon unflavored yogurt (regular, low-, or nonfat) into the top (the place where the grounds go) of a drip coffeemaker lined with filter paper and set in the top of the glass coffee carafe. Cover with plastic food wrap and refrigerate overnight. Discard the liquid that drains into the carafe [or save to use in soups, salad dressings, sauces, meatloaves. —JA]. Invert the yogurt cheese in a small container, cover, and refrigerate until needed.

—GARY GOLDBERG

643. "Hold" the butter and sour cream by mixing yogurt cheese with minced chives, scallion tops, or fresh dill; seasoning with salt and pepper; and spooning into baked potatoes.

—GARY GOLDBERG

OR

644. Whisk yogurt cheese into Caesar salad dressing as an emulsifier in place of raw egg.

—GARY GOLDBERG

OR

645. Use in place of sour cream in green goddess dressing.

—JA

OR

646. Spoon over fresh berries and drizzle with honey for a quick and delicious dessert.

—GARY GOLDBERG

OR

647. Sweeten to taste (either with superfine sugar or artifical sweetener), flavor with vanilla (or lemon or orange juice and finely grated zest, or a little Grand Marnier, sweet port, or Madeira wine), and use as a

topping for any fresh fruit dessert, even for slices of angel cake.

—JA

648. For the world's fastest low-fat peach ice cream, empty a 20-ounce package solidly frozen, unsweetened peach slices into a food processor fitted with the metal chopping blade. Add 2 tablespoons *each* Grand Marnier, frozen orange juice and limeade concentrates, 6 individual-size packets aspartame sweetener (or ⅓ cup superfine sugar), ½ teaspoon almond extract, and ¼ teaspoon ground nutmeg. With the motor running, trickle ¾ to 1 cup evaporated skim milk down the feed tube (for firm or soft ice cream) and churn 2 to 3 minutes until smooth. Serve at once. Makes 6 servings.

—JA

649. For a quick, light dessert: Use top-quality, freshly squeezed grapefruit juice, orange juice, or lemonade, and add enough liqueur to flavor it (about 1 tablespoon per cup). Pour shallow layers in nonaluminum pans and freeze, stirring occasionally. Serve with biscotti or butter cookies.

—CAROL GUTHRIE DOVELL

650. For a fast, fat-reduced fruit sauce, blend equal parts of light sour cream and heavy cream with a spoonful of sugar or honey and a drop or two of vanilla extract. Spoon over fresh or frozen berries and sprinkle with cinnamon.

—JEANNE VOLTZ

651. Make a light topping for ice cream or frozen yogurt by stirring 2 to 3 tablespoons peach preserves and the juice of 1 lemon into 3 cups of sliced fresh or frozen peaches. Stir in superfine sugar to taste.

—JEANNE VOLTZ

652. Use unsweetened cocoa powder in frozen desserts, puddings, and pie fillings instead of chocolate. If you choose the dark, deeply flavored Dutch-process cocoa powder, 1 tablespoon will equal the chocolate flavor of a 1-ounce square (and trim saturated fats as much as 75 percent).

—JA

ALSO

653. Use cocoa powder in soufflés instead of solid chocolate.

—STEVEN RAICHLEN

654. Partially frozen evaporated skim milk whips up like heavy cream. Also keep a can in the refrigerator for low-fat additions to desserts and fresh fruit frappés.

—ROZANNE GOLD

ALSO

655. Substitute evaporated skim milk for cream in frozen desserts, puddings, pie fillings, and sauces. It's

especially compatible with caramel, butterscotch, and chocolate.

—JA

656. Choose open-face pies over double-crusted ones.

—Conventional kitchen wisdom

657. For a practically fat-free crust, substitute frozen phyllo pastry for traditional pie crust. Thaw as directed, lift two leaves from the stack and center in a 9- or 10-inch pie pan sprayed with nonstick cooking spray. Lay two more leaves in pan at right angles to first, then two more on the bias to fill gaps, then two more so pan is fully lined. With damp paper toweling, gently press phyllo into pan. Take care removing towel so you don't tear the phyllo. Fill pie as directed, then to "crisp" the crust, bake the pie 10 minutes on a heavy-duty baking sheet, preheated with the oven to 425° F. Finish baking the pie, still on the baking sheet, at 350° F. or as recipe directs.

—JA

658. Choose angel cakes instead of butter cakes. They contain zero fat.

—Conventional kitchen wisdom

659. Use prune purée or applesauce in place of shortening or butter in brownies, muffins, and simple cakes.

—STEVEN RAICHLEN

ALSO

660. Puréed cooked beets can be substituted measure for measure for the fat in brownies, chocolate cupcakes, or loaf cakes.

—JA

AND

661. Canned solid-pack pumpkin can take the place of fat in gingerbread. It not only slashes fat, cholesterol, and calories but also adds a hefty dose of beta-carotene.

—JA

Presentation/ Serving

662. When planning a meal, always visualize how the food will look on a plate. Aim for a contrast of color (reds, greens and yellows, for example), of shape (rounds and squares and slivers) and textures both coarse and smooth.

— JA

663. Make sure the purée you are using to create a pattern on a soup is the same consistency as the soup. If heavier, it will sink when you try to feather it.

—Leah Stewart

664. To puddle sauce or gravy smoothly on a plate, ladle a bit in the center, then with the bowl of the ladle and a fast circular motion, spread sauce right to the rim.

—*Old chef's trick*

665. To jazz up a baked meat loaf, place crusty-side-up on a heatproof platter, then score the top at 1-inch

intervals, slicing clear across and making the cuts 1 inch deep. Tuck triangular slices of American or Swiss cheese (sandwich slices halved on the diagonal) into the cuts, letting their points overlap on top of the loaf. Warm about 2 minutes in a moderate oven—just until the cheese begins to melt, then serve.

—Conventional kitchen wisdom

666. Bake a party meatloaf in a ring mold, then fill the center with green peas, creamed mushrooms, or a bowl of sauce.

—JA

667. To give plates a "designer" look, stand chops on their rib ends, or prop against a little hillock of rice, potatoes or colorful vegetables. Fish and fowl fillets prop beautifully, too.

—Old chef's trick

668. Give parsley a rest by using other greens to garnish: carrot tops, peppergrass sprouts, fresh bay or nasturtium leaves, rose or lemon geranium leaves, sprigs of fresh chervil, cilantro or tarragon, little bundles of fresh chives, about-to-bloom sprigs of basil, chives or thyme, even baby scallions with frilled tops (to "frill," julienne the green part of each scallion, then chill in ice water).

—Conventional kitchen wisdom

669. Use two forks when serving soufflé to keep it from falling.

—SIMONE BECK, adapted from *Food and Friends* (Viking Penguin)

670. To heat a serving bowl for pasta, place a large heatproof bowl in the sink and set a colander in the bowl. When the pasta is done, pour it immediately into the colander and lift the colander to drain the cooking water into the bowl. Tip the bowl to empty it, put pasta and sauce in the warm bowl, toss, and serve.

—MICHELE SCICOLONE

671. For fancily shaped rice "cakes," spray individual star, ring or fluted gelatin molds with nonstick cooking spray, fill with cooked rice, then compact by setting a same-size, same-shape mold (coated on the outside with nonstick spray) on top of the rice and pressing hard. Unmold rice "cakes" directly onto platter or plates. The same technique works well with chopped cooked spinach that has been drained bone-dry.

—*Conventional kitchen wisdom*

672. For uniform crêpes and pancakes, use measuring cups designed for dry ingredients (a ¼-cup measure for medium-size flapjacks, a ⅓-cup measure for big ones, and a 2-tablespoon coffee measure for crêpes). Grease the cups inside and out so the batter will slip out easily. And to keep the batter from dripping en route to the

griddle, scrape the bottom of the measure on the rim of the mixing bowl.

—JEANNE LESEM

673. To make scrambled eggs creamy, stir in 1 slightly beaten egg and 1 tablespoon of butter a few seconds before you remove the pan from the heat.

—MARION CUNNINGHAM

674. For a beautiful and delicious compound butter, mix minced shallots and chives into the butter, then shape into a log in plastic wrap. Refrigerate until firm, then roll the log in a mixture of coarsely chopped edible flower petals and herbs of your choice. (Try rose, pansy, chive blossoms, dill, and Italian parsley in different combinations.) Rewrap the log in plastic and refrigerate (or freeze). To serve, slice into ¼-inch-thick rounds.

—KATHY CASEY

675. For pretty salad croutons, cut soft bread with a small disc cutter. Brush with butter, arrange on cookie sheet, and bake in 350° F. oven for 20 minutes or until brown.

—DARINA ALLEN

676. Parmesan can be shaved in large curls with a vegetable peeler and placed decoratively atop green salads or chunky pastas.

—LYNNE ROSSETTO KASPER,
adapted from *The Splendid Table*
(William Morrow)

ALSO

677. Use a vegetable peeler to make paper-thin slices of mushrooms or cucumbers to use as decorative toppings or in salads.

—JANE KIRBY

AND

678. Use it to strip off spirals of citrus zest or tomato skin, which can be twirled into "roses" and used as garnishes.

—JA

679. Prettier than radish roses: Cherry tomato flowers. To make, place tomatoes upside-down on cutting board, then cutting to within ¼ inch of the bottom, quarter or divide into sixths. Spread the petals and place the cherry tomato flowers strategically on platter or individual plates.

—JA

680. Nothing brightens a plate faster than a bit of red. And nothing lifts cherry tomatoes from the humdrum to the haute faster than a quick sauté in olive oil and a sprinkling of finely slivered fresh basil, spinach or watercress. Instead of using the tomatoes as a garnish, allow 6 per person for a side dish that's as nutritious as it is colorful.

—*Old chef's trick*

681. Learn to use edible blossoms as garnishes—wild mustard flowers, for example, to dress up an open-face tomato sandwich, or bright nasturtiums tossed into a green salad.

> —DEBORAH MADISON, adapted
> from *The Savory Way* (Bantam)

682. For an unusual garnish, fry parsley for a few seconds in deep hot fat and drain on paper towels.

> —SIMONE BECK, adapted from
> *Food and Friends* (Viking
> Penguin)

683. For perfectly clean-cut slices of cheesecakes or buttercream-frosted cakes, briefly run a thin-bladed slicing knife through an open flame, then cut. Wipe the blade and reheat between cuts.

> —BEN and KAREN BARKER

OR

684. Run the knife under very warm water between cuts.

> —DEBORAH MINTCHEFF

OR

685. Use dental floss, held very taut (this works best for cheesecake).

> —ROSE LEVY BERANBAUM

686. To cut a jelly roll neatly, loop a 15-inch length of heavy white thread underneath the roll, bring the ends up on top, cross and pull tighter and tighter until a slice is freed.

—*Conventional kitchen wisdom*

687. If you need finely ground nuts of uniform size for decorating cakes and cookies, sift the ground nuts.

—JO ANN BRETT

688. To make the best and prettiest chocolate shavings, use white or milk chocolate; these are softer and curl better.

—NICK MALGIERI

689. Paint paper muffin cups with melted bittersweet chocolate, chill until firm, then peel off the paper. Fill the chocolate dessert cups with pudding or sweetened sliced berries and serve on a chilled silver or pewter platter so the chocolate stays cold and the cups hold their shape.

—DIONE LUCAS, adapted from *The Dione Lucas Book of French Cooking*, with Marion Gorman (Little Brown)

690. When packing a gift box of cookies, slip in a bit of dried lemon or orange peel or a vanilla bean.

—DIETER G. SCHORNER

691. For a prettier Christmas punch bowl, slice green-skinned apples ½ inch thick from stem to core. Then using star, diamond or fluted round cookie cutters, remove the cores. Dip apple slices in lemon juice, then float in a bowl of red punch.

—JOANNE HAYES

692. Freeze some of the party punch in a ring mold, then float it in the punch bowl. This way the ice won't water down the punch.

—*Conventional kitchen wisdom*

ALSO

693. Freeze cubes of lemon, lime, or orangeade. They do wonders for iced tea.

—JA

694. To unmold a frozen dessert or gelatin mixture neatly, loosen around the edge of the mold with a knife tip and invert on a platter. Then, with your hair dryer set on high, blast it for a few seconds from a distance of about 6 to 8 inches.

—*Conventional kitchen wisdom*

695. So you can adjust the position of a fancy frozen bombe or gelatin mold on its platter, wet the platter before you do the unmolding.

—JA

696. To "paint" the sauce on a dessert plate, pool a little of the sauce in the bottom of a plate, then with a second sauce of contrasting color in a squirt bottle with a fine tip, make a series of concentric circles in the first sauce. Then at regular intervals, draw a knife tip or poultry pin across the sauce rings, creating a wavy effect.

—JA

697. To "paint" hearts, squirt the second sauce into a ring of dots, spacing them about an inch apart. Stick a knife tip or poultry pin in the center of a dot, pull it to the right or left, up or down, forming a heart. For two-toned hearts, place a smaller dot of contrasting color inside each large dot.

—JA

698. For the ideal disposable pastry bag, use heavy-duty, quart-sized self-sealing plastic bags fitted with a neoprene cake decorating coupler and tip. The filling can't work its way out of these bags because they're sealed tight.

—ROSE LEVY BERANBAUM

699. If you're inexperienced at using a pastry bag, stand it in a tall, heavy glass to fill. To keep out the air, always push the contents down in the bag as you fill it. And continue to twist the bag down on the contents as you pipe. The minute you allow air in the bag, it becomes flaccid and you lose control.

—LEAH STEWART

700. Always pipe the filling completely out of a pastry bag before you refill it. If you try to fill a half-empty bag there will be too many air pockets and the piping will not go smoothly.

—NANCY SILVERTON, adapted from
Desserts (HarperCollins)

701. To save time, pipe rosettes or dollops of whipped cream onto foil-covered baking sheets and freeze. Transfer to self-sealing plastic bags, label and date, and store in the freezer. Then all you need do to dress up a dessert is top each portion with a rosette or dollop of frozen whipped cream. They will thaw in 10 minutes or less.

—*Conventional kitchen wisdom*

702. To center an inscription on a cake ("Happy Birthday" or "Welcome Home"), first write the message on paper and measure its length in inches. (Counting letters won't work because some take more space than others.) Divide the length in half to determine the center of the inscription and mark it on the paper; then mark the center of the cake top. Align the center of the inscription with the center of the cake, and mark or trace the position of the letters on the cake before piping on the icing.

—FLO BRAKER

703. When dusting cakes, try cocoa instead of confectioners' sugar. Or ground cinnamon. Or very finely ground toasted almonds or hazelnuts.

—JA

AND

704. Instead of sifting confectioners' sugar, cocoa, cinnamon or ground nuts through comercial paper doilies, let your imagination soar by making your own templates. Trace designs on manilla file folders, then cut out using a razor-sharp box cutter or mat knife.

—JA

705. For a festive touch, dust mint sprigs lightly with confectioners' sugar before using to garnish a dessert plate or platter.

—JA

LEFTOVERS

706. Plan meals with leftovers in mind. For example, a stew can emerge later in the week as meat pie. Or if frozen, several months later. Or if curry powder is mixed in along with a little chutney and ground hot red peppers, the stew can reappear as curry, ladled steaming hot over boiled rice.

—JA

707. Slice leftover roast and lay the slices in a single layer on a cookie sheet lined with plastic wrap. Cover with aluminum foil and freeze. Once frozen, slip slices into a self-sealing plastic bag and return to freezer. Remove slices as needed and thaw in microwave.

—BEN ETHERIDGE

708. Combine leftover vegetables and purée, shape into patties, crumb with crushed potato chips, and bake for a next-day meal.

—ELIZABETH TERRY

709. Package leftover rice in 1-cup portions and store in the freezer for up to 3 months. To reheat, add 2 tablespoons liquid and microwave at 100 percent power for 2 minutes.

—BONNIE TANDY LEBLANG

OR

710. Shape the rice into pancakes, layer between sheets of foil or plastic food wrap, and freeze. They need only to be browned in butter or oil and served as an accompaniment to any meat that has lots of gravy.

—JA

711. To reheat leftover pasta without drying it out, warm it in a microwave. Or bundle tightly in foil, then heat in a preheated 350° F. oven for 15 to 20 minutes.

—JULIA DELLA CROCE, adapted
from *Pasta Classica* (Chronicle)

712. Crêpes, whether sweet or savory, are marvelous for using up leftovers. Just fill them however you please to serve next day or freeze for later use.

—DARINA ALLEN

713. Cool leftover French toast on a wire rack, then freeze it in single layers, and repack in self-sealing plastic bags. Pop in your toaster to reheat.

—AMERICAN EGG BOARD

714. Mash leftover cooked dried beans and freeze in ice cube trays, then repack in freezer container or self-

sealing bags. Add the cubes directly to soup, sauce, or stew as a thickener and flavor enhancer.

—BONNIE TANDY LEBLANG

OR

715. Save any leftover cooked dried beans—white, black, pinto, pink, red kidney, chick-peas—and use as the basis of a cold salad.

—JA

OR

716. Mash leftover dried beans with minced garlic and enough vinaigrette or yogurt for a good dipping consistency. Season to taste with dill or marjoram and hot red pepper sauce, and serve as a cocktail dip.

—*Conventional kitchen wisdom*

717. Recycle vegetable cooking water in soups and sauces.

—*Conventional kitchen wisdom*

718. Don't toss out a can of tomato paste after using just a spoonful. Instead, line a dinner plate with wax paper and drop tomato paste by teaspoonfuls [or tablespoonfuls] onto the paper, spacing them well apart. Freeze until firm, then transfer to a self-sealing plastic bag and store in freezer until needed.

—LYNNE ROSSETTO KASPER

OR

719. Freeze leftover tomato paste in ice cube trays. It's best to cover the paste with a thin film of water before freezing.

—BARBARA KAFKA

720. After you've grated a chunk of Parmesan or romano cheese, don't discard the hard, inedible rind. Wrap it well, refrigerate, then use it to add extraordinary depth and flavor to your next batch of chicken, vegetable, lentil, or bean soup.

—DANNY MEYER

OR

721. Save rinds of Parmesan, scraps of Cheddar, and bits of Brie. When you have enough, grind them in a food processor with a leek or onion, some garlic, white wine, and light chicken stock. This is a simple formula for the *fromage fort* of Lyon, traditionally served with toasted bread. It keeps well and is a great cocktail spread.

—PRISCILLA MARTEL

722. Recycle hard, dried-out cheese by grating it in a food processor or by hand. Pack it loosely in a covered container and refrigerate or freeze for use in macaroni and cheese or for casserole toppings, or add beer or port wine and whip into a spread.

—JEANNE LESEM

723. Create a "cheese bank" by grating leftover hard cheeses (Swiss, Cheddar, Parmesan) and storing in a plastic bag in the fridge. Make withdrawals as needed.

—JULIA CHILD, adapted from *Julia Child & Company* (Knopf)

724. Freeze leftover egg whites, one per ice cube tray compartment, then pop out and store in self-sealing plastic bags.

—MERYLE EVANS

725. How do you use frozen egg whites? First thaw, then use when breading a variety of food. Or beat 1 egg white with 1 tablespoon cold water and use to glaze yeast breads before they go into the oven (they will emerge glistening). Or mix into scrambled eggs and frittatas, muffins, and simple cakes. As a rule, two extra whites per recipe is plenty. In baked goods, substitute two thawed frozen whites for one whole egg. Never use thawed frozen egg whites for angel cakes or soufflés. They'll never whip to stratospheric heights and give you the volume you want.

—JA

726. Make your own melba toast or pumpernickel crisps with leftover bread. Partially freeze uncut portions and slice very thin with a sharp knife, then bake at a low temperature until crunchy.

—ROZANNE GOLD

727. Leftover crusty bread is great for Italian bread soups and as an accompaniment for salads.

—CAROL FIELD, adapted from *The Italian Baker* (HarperCollins)

728. For a lively taste, use leftover sweet pickle juice in deviling eggs, or mix into meatloaves or meatballs.

—JA

729. Don't pour canned or frozen fruit syrups down the drain. Use to sweeten fresh berries or fruit compotes, or add to bottled fruit drinks.

—JA

OR

730. Combine with other fruit juices and use as part of the liquid in fruit gelatins.

—JA

OR

731. Use to glaze baked ham, roast chicken or turkey, or browned meatballs.

—JA

732. Jazz up leftover biscuits by splitting, tucking in a cube of Cheddar or Swiss cheese, and reheating in the microwave or oven.

—*Conventional kitchen wisdom*

Or

733. Split, brush lightly with olive oil, sprinkle with freshly grated Parmesan, and broil until tipped with brown.

—JA

Or

734. Crumble and freeze in self-sealing plastic bags to use as cobbler toppings later on. Or to add to poultry stuffing.

—JA

735. To freshen stale rolls, seal in a paper bag, sprinkle the bag with water, and heat 10 to 15 minutes at 350° F.

—JA

736. To heat leftover tortillas, grease a skillet lightly with oil and place over medium heat. Dip tortillas in water and quickly steam-sauté them on both sides.

—GRAHAM KERR, adapted from
Graham Kerr's Smart Cooking
(Doubleday)

Or

737. Spritz the tortillas with water from a mister or spray bottle, then roll them about on a hot griddle until warm and supple.

—JIM FOBEL

738. To make leftover fruit pie taste "just-baked," wrap in foil and warm 10 minutes in a 350° F. oven.

—*Conventional kitchen wisdom*

739. Use leftover pie or tart pastry to make pastry cases for hors d'oeuvre. If you like, freeze and save for a special occasion.

—Dione Lucas, adapted from *The Dione Lucas Book of French Cooking*, with Marion Gorman (Little, Brown)

Or

740. Reroll, cut in fancy shapes, sprinkle with cinnamon sugar, and bake. The kids will love them.

—*Conventional kitchen wisdom*

741. Freeze leftover coffee and tea in ice cube trays. Use cubes to cool down iced beverages without diluting them.

—Beverly Barbour

HERBS, SPICES & FLAVOR ENHANCERS

742. Keep a testing spoon by your stove. When you want to taste, use the cooking (stirring) spoon to fill your tasting spoon. (Many chefs carry a tasting spoon in the pocket of their chef's coat.)

—*Conventional kitchen wisdom*

743. When something is to be served cold—pâté, ice cream, cold soups—pump up the seasonings. Cold numbs the palate.

—*Conventional kitchen wisdom*

744. Cold water brings out flavor, hot water seals it in. Thus, always start a stock with cold water.

—DARINA ALLEN

745. Kosher salt, favored by many because of its freedom from chemicals and additives, has big crystals that won't shake out of ordinary salt cellars. Designate

a spare pepper mill as a salt mill and twist salt directly onto food at the table.

—MARIE BIANCO

746. Keep salt in a small bowl. When you season, use your fingers instead of a shaker; you'll be less likely to overseason.

—DARINA ALLEN

747. Salt won't dissolve in oil, so when preparing a vinaigrette, always dissolve the salt in the vinegar or lemon juice, then whisk in the oil.

—PATRICIA WELLS, adapted from *Patricia Wells' Trattoria* (William Morrow)

748. Use a bouillon cube in stock rather than salt (2 cubes for 6 to 8 quarts liquid). The bouillon adds all the salt you need, enhances flavor, and contains too little MSG to trigger possible allergic reactions.

—MADELINE KAMMAN, adapted from *Madeleine Cooks Chicken* (Breger Video, Inc.)

749. Enrich commercial balsamic vinegars by adding a generous pinch of dark brown sugar per tablespoon of vinegar, then use as a salt substitute on cooked meats, fish, fowl, and vegetables.

—LYNNE ROSSETTO KASPER, adapted from *The Splendid Table* (William Morrow)

750. Instead of chopping up fresh basil yourself, try substituting a commercially bottled basil oil to sauté zucchini, onions, and other vegetables as well as fish or poultry fillets.

—CAROL HADDIX

751. A touch of salt enlivens the flavor of yogurt.

—DARINA ALLEN

752. To desalinate overly salty brined black olives, simmer about 10 minutes in water and drain well.

—JULIA CHILD, adapted from *Julia Child & More Company* (Knopf)

753. To tell how much ground pepper you're adding to a recipe, grind it directly into your hand, then add.

—ARTHUR SCHWARTZ, adapted from *Soup Suppers* (HarperCollins)

OR

754. Grind peppercorns in a small electric coffee grinder and store the pepper in little crocks or bowls at the stove or table. Store coarse salt in separate bowls alongside the pepper. This makes it easy to reach in and get as much as you need of either.

—MARTHA STEWART, adapted from syndicated TV series, "Martha Stewart Living"

755. In a special pepper grinder reserved for this purpose, mix about 70 to 80 percent whole black or white

peppercorns with 10 to 15 percent each of allspice and whole coriander. (Vary the proportions according to taste.) Or add a few Szechuan peppercorns, either to the mixture described or to spice up plain black peppercorns. Use these flavored peppers instead of salt on simply prepared fish or chicken.

—Cornelius O'Donnell

756. To add cayenne to a dish, use the tip of a small paring knife. For other seasonings, use your fingers.

—Darina Allen

757. Rather than buying ground or powdered spices, buy them whole, then roast them in a hot dry saucepan for 2 to 3 minutes and grind them yourself in a coffee grinder. This greatly improves their flavor.

—Gray Kunz

Or

758. Load in a peppermill and grind directly over your food.

—Darina Allen

759. Sauté *ground* spices in oil to intensify their flavor or roast them briefly in a pie tin in a 350° F. oven.

—*Conventional kitchen wisdom*

760. When you use commercial curry powder, combine two or more brands—each has a different mix of spices.

—DIONE LUCAS, adapted from *The Dione Lucas Book of French Cooking*, with Marion Gorman (Little, Brown)

761. For richer flavor, season chicken 24 hours before roasting and store in the refrigerator.

—THOMAS KELLER

762. To bring out the flavor of such bland birds as Cornish hens, roast under a light coverlet of a good, nutty, shredded Gruyère or Gruyère mixed with a little shredded mozzarella.

—JULIA CHILD, adapted from *Julia Child & More Company* (Knopf)

763. To add zing to seafood, poultry, or steaks, dust them with spices before sautéing. Try different flavors: curry powder, garam masala, chili powder, ground ancho chili powder. Harmonize flavors with a little salt and sugar.

—SALLY SCHNEIDER

764. A French grandmother's tip: When cooking French lentils, add a teaspoon of vinegar and a sugar cube to the cooking water.

—PATRICIA WELLS, adapted from *Patricia Wells' Trattoria* (William Morrow)

765. Cheesecloth, the traditional wrapping for *bouquet garni*, can be hard to find; foil's a good substitute. Spread out a generous square of foil and lay upon it 2 bay leaves, 2 sprigs of thyme (or 1 teaspoon dried), 4 sprigs of fresh parsley, 2 cloves, 2 allspice berries, and 10 black peppercorns. Fold the foil to seal shut, then pierce the package all over with a fork to release flavors. Drop in the dish to be flavored.

—STEVEN RAICHLEN

OR

766. Place *bouquet garni* ingredients in a tea ball and suspend in a soup or stew, hooking the end of the chain over the rim of the pot.

—JA

767. To add more spices or herbs to a simmering stew, put the desired flavoring on a leaf of soft lettuce, secure it with toothpicks, and drop it into the pot. The mild lettuce adds no flavor but the hot stock breaks down its membranes, allowing the liquid to wash through the herbs or spices and absorb their flavor. A much easier method than using cheesecloth!

—CAROL CUTLER

768. Before adding a *bouquet garni* to the pot, bruise it slightly with a mallet or the back of a knife to release the herbs' volatile oils.

—GRAHAM KERR, adapted from
Graham Kerr's Smart Cooking
(Doubleday)

769. Self-sealing bags of various sizes are invaluable for marinating meat, poultry, and vegetables because they take up very little space in the refrigerator; a jiggle of the bag is all it takes to ensure that the marinade is evenly distributed; and no cleanup is necessary afterwards.

—BETTY ROSBOTTOM

770. Use light (slightly sweeter) soy sauce for marinades; use dark (slightly heavier) soy sauce for cooking and sauces.

—KEN HOM, adapted from *A Guide to Chinese Cooking* (Videocraft Classics, NYC)

771. Add cornstarch to a marinade to make it stick better.

—KEN HOM, adapted from *A Guide to Chinese Cooking* (Videocraft Classics, NYC)

772. Sometimes canned baby corn, bamboo shoots, water chestnuts, and straw mushrooms have an undesirable metallic taste. To remove, drain well, blanch in boiling water 1 minute, then rinse in cool water.

—MARTIN YAN

773. If you add just a few teaspoons of cream to a sauce made with milk, it will taste as though made entirely from cream.

—DIONE LUCAS, adapted from *The Dione Lucas Book of French Cooking*, with Marion Gorman (Little, Brown)

774. To preserve the sweetness and flavor and reduce the bitterness of sun-dried tomatoes and dried mushrooms, reconstitute by soaking in cool or cold water.

—MARY BETH CLARK

775. For freshly cleaned, beautifully colored chopped parsley, wrap it in the corner of a sturdy paper towel, rinse under cold water, and wring it out.

—GRAHAM KERR, adapted from *Graham Kerr's Smart Cooking* (Doubleday)

776. To get the most flavor from fresh parsley, stem it, leaving only the leaves. Put the leaves in a deep bowl and snip them with sharp scissors. This way they won't turn to mush as they do when chopped with a knife or in a food processor.

—PATRICIA WELLS, adapted from *Patricia Wells' Trattoria* (William Morrow)

777. Fresh parsley chopped with dried herbs freshens their flavor and aroma.

—BERT GREENE, adapted from *The Vegetable Lover's Video* (Videocraft Classics, NYC)

778. To revive the flavor of dried herbs you intend to use in an uncooked recipe such as salad or salsa, mix the herbs with lemon juice and/or chopped onion and let stand 15 minutes.

—NAO HAUSER

779. Perk up white rice by cooking in chicken broth with a pinch of crumbled dried thyme, marjoram, rosemary, or basil in the cooking water.

—JA

780. When serving braised fennel, garnish it with fennel fronds—that's what holds the licorice flavor.

—BERT GREENE, adapted from *The Vegetable Lover's Video* (Videocraft Classics, NYC)

781. For a different and delicious pesto, substitute arugula for basil.

—LEAH STEWART

782. To zip up a minestrone, add a dollop of pesto.

—CAROL FIELD, adapted from *Italy in Small Bites* (William Morrow)

783. Add a tablespoon of balsamic vinegar to pesto.

—LYNNE ROSSETTO KASPER, adapted from *The Splendid Table* (William Morrow)

784. Flavored oils, especially those flavored with basil or garlic, give extraordinary lift to many dishes. Drizzle basil-flavored oil over sliced tomatoes and mozzarella. Use roasted garlic-flavored oil in a quick sauté of potatoes. Experiment with other flavors.

—PEGGY KATALINICH

785. A medium garlic clove, minced, equals about ⅛ teaspoon.

—GILROY'S FINEST GARLIC

786. To preserve minced garlic, separate whole bulb into cloves, smash with blade of cleaver to loosen, and remove the peel. Mince the peeled garlic fine, place in a glass jar, and cover with peanut oil (for Chinese cooking) or olive oil (for Western). Store in the coldest part of the refrigerator and, to play it safe, use within two weeks.

—EILEEN YIN-FEI LO

787. To tame the flavor of garlic, blanch it 3 to 4 minutes in boiling water. Blanching also makes it easier to peel.

—JULIA CHILD, adapted from *Julia Child & More Company* (Knopf)

788. When a recipe directs you to add oil, garlic, and onions to a pan, always add garlic last. This keeps it from burning.

—BERT GREENE, adapted from *The Vegetable Lover's Video* (Videocraft Classics, NYC)

789. Roasted garlic is wonderfully sweet and nutty and it's good to have a supply on hand to use in recipes. Here's how to prepare it: Roast several unpeeled heads of garlic, tossed in olive oil, in a 350° F. oven about 25 minutes until softened. Peel the garlic, purée,

place in a glass preserving jar, and cover with a film of olive oil. Stored in the coldest part of the refrigerator, it keeps well. Use within two weeks.

—BEN and KAREN BARKER

790. Use garlic purée for a softer, richer garlic flavor in marinades and vinaigrettes. Add to mashed potatoes, to sauces in lieu of butter, to risotto or soft polenta. Or, use as a body liniment to ease aches and pains.

—BEN and KAREN BARKER

791. The longer you cook garlic, the more delicate its flavor becomes. If you like a subtle taste, keep cloves whole or cut in large pieces and use in long-simmering stews and soups. For stronger flavor, purée, crush, or mince and add to foods just before serving.

—GILROY'S FINEST GARLIC

792. Mash garlic cloves into butter (use 6 cloves per stick), add chopped chives or parsley, and salt lightly. Form into logs, wrap in plastic, and freeze. Slice as needed to melt on broiled steaks or burgers, mix into fresh vegetables, or spread on bread.

—GILROY'S FINEST GARLIC

793. For garlic-flavored potato chips, place a peeled clove in a bag of chips, seal, and let stand several hours.

—GILROY'S FINEST GARLIC

794. For garlic popcorn, add a peeled clove to the popping oil.

—GILROY'S FINEST GARLIC

795. Freeze a peeled or unpeeled "hand" of ginger. While still frozen, grate or cut into small cubes and crush in garlic press for spicy ginger juice. (Freezing releases these juices and makes the ginger easier to crush.)

—CAROL CUTLER

796. Prepare ginger juice for use in recipes in two stages: First peel fresh ginger, chop it in a food processor, and freeze in a tightly covered container. When ready for juice, defrost the ginger and place it in four layers of cheesecloth or a man's cotton handkerchief; then squeeze this makeshift bag over a bowl.

—JEANNE LESEM

OR

797. Make ginger juice (no longer than a day in advance) by peeling a large slice of fresh ginger, grating it on a single-panel hand grater, packing it into a garlic press, and squeezing out the juice.

—EILEEN YIN-FEI LO

798. For a quick snap of ginger flavor, cut fresh, unpeeled ginger into 1- to 2-inch pieces, place in a self-sealing plastic bag, and freeze. Defrost as needed, squeeze out the juice, and discard the mushy pulp.

—CAROL CUTLER

799. Because fresh ginger is quite acidic, it should be blanched before it's added to milk or cream. Otherwise, it may curdle.

—NANCY SILVERTON, adapted from
Desserts (HarperCollins)

800. Zip up old-fashioned gingerbread by mixing in about ¼ cup minced fresh ginger and the finely grated zest of an orange.

—JA

801. Grate a little fresh ginger and nutmeg into your next fruit compote or salad. They perk up ambrosia, too.

—JA

802. Store fresh ginger in vodka or sherry wine—it improves the flavor of both ginger and spirits. Or plant a ginger root in potting soil.

—BERT GREENE, adapted from *The
Vegetable Lover's Video*
(Videocraft Classics, NYC)

803. To add interest to steamed lemon pudding, add a bit of fresh rosemary.

—MICHAEL ROBERTS, adapted
from *Secret Ingredients* (Bantam)

804. Try heightening the flavor of any lemon dessert (chess pie, cake, sorbet, ice cream) with lemon grass, lemon verbena, lemon geranium, or lavender.

—JA

805. Add a tablespoon of freshly grated horseradish to a bowl of mashed potatoes.

—JAMES VILLAS

806. Add a bit of lemon juice just before serving cream of mushroom soup to bring out its full flavor.

—WOLFGANG PUCK, adapted from *Spago Cooking with Wolfgang Puck* (Warner Home Video, Inc.)

807. Drizzle balsamic vinegar into bean or vegetable soups.

—LYNNE ROSSETTO KASPER, adapted from *The Splendid Table* (William Morrow)

808. When chopping lemon or orange peel, add 2 tablespoons sugar from the recipe you are making to capture and carry the citrus flavor.

—ELIZABETH TERRY

809. Bury strips of lemon or orange zest in cannisters of sugar (either granulated or confectioners') to give the sugar a delicate citrus taste.

—JA

810. Next time you make a meatloaf or meatballs, slip in a little finely grated orange or lemon zest.

—JA

811. You'll get added flavor as well as protection from discoloration if you sprinkle avocado with lime juice instead of lemon juice.

—CRAIG CLAIBORNE, adapted from
*Craig Claiborne's New York Times
Video Cookbook* (Warner Home
Video)

812. If you can't find orange flower water and need it for a recipe, macerate dried orange peel for 24 hours in sweet white wine.

—SIMONE BECK, adapted from
Food and Friends (Viking
Penguin)

813. Make your own special mushroom powder to enrich sauces and soups by using your blender or food processor to reduce dried morels and/or porcini (*cèpes*) to a fine powder. Store in a tightly sealed jar.

—KATHY CASEY

814. Mushrooms and hazelnuts have a special affinity for one another, so sauté mushrooms in hazelnut oil instead of butter or olive oil.

—JA

815. For a potato salad with superb nutty flavor, bake the potatoes instead of boiling them.

—JA

816. Add a few spoonfuls of balsamic vinegar to potato salad or coleslaw or sprinkle over tomato salad with mozzarella and chopped fresh basil.

—LYNNE ROSSETTO KASPER,
adapted from *The Splendid Table*
(William Morrow)

817. To approximate the rich nutty flavor of clarified butter, add a touch of toasted sesame seed oil to another light-flavored oil. (A "touch" is 1/16 part—1 ounce to 1 pint for instance.)

—GRAHAM KERR, adapted from
Graham Kerr's Smart Cooking
(Doubleday)

OR

818. Add 1/16 part hazelnut oil.

—JA

819. Always add extracts and other flavorings to the butter, rather than to other ingredients in a recipe. Butter picks up flavor more readily.

—JIM DODGE, adapted from
Baking with Jim Dodge, with
Elaine Ratner (Simon &
Schuster)

820. Toss a grating of bitter chocolate into chili to give it body and mellow the flavors. It's what Mexicans do with a *mole*.

—JAMES BEARD, adapted from
Simple Foods (Macmillan)

OR

821. Try thickening a spicy sauce with a little un-sweetened cocoa powder.

—JA

822. Vanilla underscores the sweetness of shellfish. Try adding a drop or two to lobster soup.

—MICHAEL ROBERTS, adapted
from *Secret Ingredients* (Bantam)

823. When you heat cream for sweet custards, infuse it with a vanilla bean for more complexity of flavor. For variety, try star anise, cinnamon stick, cardamom, or citrus zest.

—DARINA ALLEN

824. A splash of Spanish sherry jazzes up ordinary canned soup.

—JAMES BEARD, adapted from
Simple Foods (Macmillan)

825. When making your next apple pie, try crumbling a little marzipan with the flour and butter. Omit the cinnamon and add a bit of lemon juice and zest.

—JA

826. Scatter a few drops of fine, aged balsamic vinegar over a simple apple tart flavored with sugar, cinnamon, and a little butter.

> —LYNNE ROSSETTO KASPER,
> adapted from *The Splendid Table*
> (William Morrow)

827. Stewing prunes in tea instead of water gives them a wonderful flavor.

> —LOUISETTE BERTHOLLE, adapted
> from *French Cuisine for All*
> (Doubleday)

AND

828. The same can be said for poaching pears in a fragrant tea (jasmine, Earl Grey, whatever you fancy).

> —MARIE SIMMONS

829. For more flavorful poached fruit, cool it in its poaching liquid.

> —LEAH STEWART

830. Use a self-sealing plastic bag filled with water to keep fruits submerged in their macerating liquid.

> —DARINA ALLEN

831. Use a few drops of artisanal balsamic vinegar to accentuate the character of fresh melon and strawberries.

> —LYNNE ROSSETTO KASPER,
> adapted from *The Splendid Table*
> (William Morrow)

S.O.S.

The Prevention & Cure

of Disasters

832. To rescue cream that you've overwhipped, gently fold in a few tablespoons of milk or unwhipped cream.

—Nick Malgieri

833. To stabilize whipped cream, add 2 tablespoons of nonfat dry milk to every cup of whipping cream *before* you whip it.

—Marion Cunningham

834. If you've overbeaten egg whites and they're too stiff, gently stir in 1 or 2 unbeaten whites to every 5 or 6 beaten whites.

—Marion Cunningham

Or

835. Add a few teaspoons of sugar and beat again briefly until smooth.

—Nancy Silverton, adapted from *Desserts* (HarperCollins)

836. In a pinch, you can hold a prepared soufflé 2 hours in the refrigerator before you bake it.

— AMERICAN EGG BOARD

837. You can never reheat a *beurre blanc* sauce without its separating, but you can keep it hot. If you need to hold it for only half an hour, cover the pan and wrap in several layers of newspaper. To hold a *beurre blanc* for as long as 2 hours, transfer to a wide-mouth thermos.

— SIMONE BECK, adapted from
Food and Friends (Viking
Penguin)

838. To keep yogurt from curdling when you add it to a hot stock, soup, or sauce, first blend a little cornstarch with the yogurt, whisk a little of the hot stock into the yogurt, then mix all into the stock and cook and stir until thickened.

— GRAHAM KERR, adapted from
Graham Kerr's Smart Cooking
(Doubleday)

839. Hollandaise curdled? You can smooth it out by vigorously whisking in 2 tablespoons boiling water.

—JA

OR

840. Set the pan of curdled sauce in an ice bath and beat hard. Rewarm in the top of a double boiler, stirring all the while.

—JA

841. When a stirred custard threatens to curdle, pour at once into a cold bowl.

—*Conventional kitchen wisdom*

842. If the custard *does* curdle, not to worry. Put through a fine sieve. Or buzz until smooth in a food processor or blender.

—JA

843. After straining custard sauce, whisk it with a rolling motion, rotating the handle between the palms of your hands. This will prevent a skin from forming on the custard's surface.

—MADELEINE KAMMAN, adapted from *Madeleine Cooks, Vol. II* (Breger Video, Inc.)

Or

844. Smooth a piece of plastic wrap flat on the surface of the sauce. This works for the entire family of starch- and egg-thickened sauces.

—JA

845. If before you add the flour, your creamed butter seems separated, warm the bottom of the mixing bowl in an inch or two of warm water for about 10 seconds, then beat again. Repeat if necessary.

—NICK MALGIERI

846. To crisp lackluster lettuce, stash the washed and dried leaves in the freezer for 2 to 3 minutes, not a second more or they'll be ruined.

—JANET BAILEY, adapted from
Keeping Food Fresh
(HarperCollins)

847. To recrisp soggy crackers, spread them on a baking sheet and warm 5 minutes in a 300° F. oven. Cool and seal in an airtight cannister or plastic bag.

—*Conventional kitchen wisdom*

848. If a few drops of water get into melting chocolate, it will stiffen. To soften again, stir in vegetable oil by teaspoonfuls.

—NANCY SILVERTON, adapted from
Desserts (HarperCollins)

849. Salvage an overbaked cake by drizzling with a simple sugar syrup spiked with a little Grand Marnier, Kahlua, Tia Maria, brandy, port, or Madeira wine.

—*Conventional kitchen wisdom*

850. If you're out of brown sugar, try substituting an equal amount of granulated sugar plus ¼ cup molasses (light or dark) for every cup of white sugar.

—ELIZABETH ALSTON

851. A recipe calls for 1 cup sour milk and you have none? No matter. Stir 1 tablespoon vinegar or lemon

juice into 1 cup whole milk. Or substitute 1 cup buttermilk.

—JA

852. If you need acidulated water and are out of lemons, dissolve 1 teaspoon sour salt in 2 quarts of water.

—*Conventional kitchen wisdom*

OR

853. Mix ½ cup white vinegar and 2 quarts of water.

—JA

854. If you have no homemade chicken stock, do as **Marcella Hazan** does: Use canned, but dilute it half-and-half with water to reduce the sodium.

—LEE FOWLER

855. Never dip into a baking powder can with a wet spoon! You'll deactivate the whole can.

—JIM DODGE, adapted from
Baking with Jim Dodge, with
Elaine Ratner (Simon &
Schuster)

856. To see whether baking powder has lost its oomph, drop ½ teaspoon into a glass of warm water. If it foams to the top, the baking powder is still active.

—JIM DODGE, adapted from
Baking with Jim Dodge, with
Elaine Ratner (Simon &
Schuster)

OR

857. To determine whether baking soda is over the hill, pour a couple of tablespoons of vinegar into a ramekin, add 1 teaspoon of baking soda, and stand back. If it froths like mad, it's good.

—JA

858. To avoid cross-contaminating food (transferring possibly harmful germs from one food to another), turn your chopping board upside down after working with meat, fish, or fowl.

—WOLFGANG PUCK, adapted from *Spago Cooking with Wolfgang Puck* (Warner Home Video, Inc.)

859. Watch the color carefully when caramelizing sugar for a sauce. If the caramel is too light, it will be too sweet; if too dark, it will be bitter. Aim for chestnut.

—DARINA ALLEN

860. If the syrup you're caramelizing is hardening too fast, stir in a few drops of lemon juice.

—LOUISETTE BERTHOLLE, adapted from *French Cuisine for All* (Doubleday)

OR

861. Microwave for a few seconds to restore the fluidity.

—ROSE LEVY BERANBAUM

862. To keep a pot from boiling over, tilt its lid so it can blow off some steam.

—*Conventional kitchen wisdom*

863. Protect yourself from grease spatter by placing a metal colander upside down over the skillet.

—*Conventional kitchen wisdom*

864. Hot water baths (*bains-marie*) can be dangerous. To lessen the risk of scalded fingers, use a bulb baster to drain the bath before lifting out the cake pan.

—ALICE MEDRICH

ALSO

865. Anchor ramekins in a hot water bath by placing them on a folded dish towel. That way they won't skitter around when you lift the hot water bath in and out of the oven.

—ANNE WILLAN, adapted from TV series "Look & Cook," PBS television.

866. Never, never pour water on flaming fat or oil— you'll spread the fire. If the fire's inside a pan, slap on the lid. If outside, turn off the heat and douse the flames by tossing on a handful of baking soda or salt.

—*Conventional kitchen wisdom*

867. The safest way to flame the contents of a pan or chafing dish: Pour a little brandy into a long-handled ladle, blaze with a match, then pour into the pan.

—Leah Stewart

868. If you burn yourself, immediately pinch your earlobe with "the same side thumb and forefinger" and hold for 3 minutes. This acupuncture/shiatsu method of first aid prevents pain and blistering.

—Katharine Kagel

Or

869. Gently apply ice to a burn to cool the fire.

—William Woys Weaver

870. Three remedies for garlic breath: Eat fresh parsley, chew on a coffee bean, eat a bowl of lime sherbet.

—Gilroy's Finest Garlic

871. A guaranteed cure for garlicky hands: Immediately after chopping raw garlic, rub your fingers thoroughly with the bowl of a stainless steel spoon under running water. Then wash your hands with soap. The metal magically neutralizes the garlic fumes!

—Gilroy's Finest Garlic

MISCELLANEOUS TIPS
Why Didn't I Think of That?

872. Use top-quality typewriter correction fluid to cover nicks, chips, and scratches on enameled ranges and refrigerators, porcelain tiles, and sinks. Works like a charm. And it comes in a variety of colors.

—JA

873. If your recipe cards are always flying around the kitchen as you cook, place a fork, tines up, in a tall glass and wedge the card between the tines.

—PATRICIA WELLS, adapted from *Patricia Wells' Trattoria* (William Morrow)

874. When your cookbook won't lie flat when opened on the counter, place a glass baking dish on the pages (you can read through the glass) or secure each side with a rubber band.

—*Conventional kitchen wisdom*

875. If you store your best silver in self-sealing plastic bags, it will tarnish much more slowly.

—*Conventional kitchen wisdom*

876. To remove pesky bottle tops and jar lids, don a pair of rubber gloves. Or twist a fat rubber band around the lid, then twist open. Works like a charm.

—Barbara Tropp

877. To keep seltzer and soda bottles from spraying all over you and the kitchen, master the trick of opening and reclosing the cap in one swift motion. Wait until the effervescence subsides, then open completely.

—Jim Fobel

878. After zesting and juicing an orange or lemon, grind the remains in your garbage disposal for their refreshing scent.

—Judith Segal

879. The best way to protect cheesecakes and tarts in the refrigerator? By topping with a pizza pan or bottom of a tart tin large enough to balance securely on the cheesecake pan.

—Dora Jonassen

880. To make iced tea that is clear and not too tannic, simply put 4 tea bags in a 2-quart pitcher of water and leave in the refrigerator for about 4 hours.

—Florence Fabricant

881. Use self-sealing plastic bags in place of more cumbersome containers when transporting food.

—Carole Lalli

199

882. Fill a strong, self-sealing plastic bag with split peas or beans. Use your homemade bean bag to practice flipping food in a skillet like a professional chef.

—LEAH STEWART

883. Homemade cookie dough, ready to bake, makes an unusual and thoughtful house gift for a weekend's visit.

—DOLORES CUSTER

EQUIPMENT
Kitchen Mechanics

884. Get the habit of using a small kitchen scale for weighing out baking ingredients. Not only is it more accurate, it's much easier than packing brown sugar into a measuring cup or scraping shortening out.

—HELEN WITTY

885. Wax paper is endlessly useful: To catch grated cheese, to place under seasoned flour for breading or spices for blackening, to tear into strips to slip under a cake you are icing, to cover a dish you are microwaving.

—LYN STALLWORTH

ALSO

886. If you line your work surface with wax paper, you can roll everything up when you're finished prepping food—egg shells, flour spills, vegetable peelings, shrimp shells, whatever—and dispose of them neatly. Best of all, the counter hardly needs a wipe.

—JA

887. Keep four to five different-sized heavy-duty tongs and ladles in a container by the stove. The tongs, in particular, are invaluable for turning, transferring, and testing for doneness.

—JAN WEIMER

888. The Chinese chef's knife is endlessly useful. With it you can slice, dice, shred, chop, cut, tenderize, and crush, depending on which part of the knife you use. You can pound meat in a crisscross pattern using the blunt edge of the knife blade. You can use the end of the handle like a mortar and pestle to crush such soft items as salted black beans. With the broad side of the blade, you can smash garlic cloves or small pieces of ginger.

—MARTIN YAN

889. Collect a large assortment of Chinese wooden paddles and spoons. Use them to save wear and tear on your good stainless steel and copper pots.

—ALAN HARDING

890. For top-quality, long-lasting utensils, buy at restaurant supply houses.

—JAN WEIMER

891. Instead of using plastic wrap to cover bowls in the microwave, cover a round heatproof glass bowl with a round heatproof glass casserole cover or with an inverted heatproof glass bowl of the same size. A

heat-resistant round glass pizza pan also works well, and the overhang makes removal and recovery both safe and easy.

—CORNELIUS O'DONNELL

892. If you use a lightweight pot for boiling pasta, water will come to its initial boil faster and will return to the boil faster, too, saving time and preventing the pasta from clumping at the bottom of the pot.

—LEAH STEWART

893. Before heating a nonstick pan, *always* coat it with nonstick vegetable cooking spray and *never* heat the pan more than 3 minutes before adding food.

—MARIE BIANCO

894. To season a cast-iron pan, wipe clean, rub well with a light, flavorless vegetable oil, and heat, uncovered, 2 hours in a 250° F. oven. Cool well before using.

—JA

895. When using a steamer insert, add marbles to the bottom of the pot and set the steamer on the marbles. Add water to just above the base of the steamer, add food, and cover. The marbles will steady the steamer and let you know—by rattling against the sides of the pot—when the pot's boiling dry.

—GRAHAM KERR, adapted from
Graham Kerr's Smart Cooking
(Doubleday)

203

896. Bamboo steamers should be washed only with water, never with soap.

—KEN HOM, adapted from *A
Guide to Chinese Cooking*
(Videocraft Classics, NYC)

897. For cooking artichokes, you need a nonreactive pan (porcelain-clad cast iron, flameproof glass, stainless steel). Artichokes will darken aluminum.

—CALIFORNIA ARTICHOKE
ADVISORY BOARD

898. To sterilize jars before filling with jams, pickles, or preserves, clean and rinse the jars and place them, open sides up and without touching, on a tray. Leave in a preheated 250° F. oven for 30 minutes. This is a much easier method than dealing with tongs and boiling water.

—DIANA STURGIS

899. Improvise an asparagus cooker from a tall fruit juice can by poking holes in its bottom and sides with an ice pick, making it virtually a sieve. Stand asparagus spears in it upright, place it in a large pot, and pour in enough boiling water to reach ⅔ of the height of the can. Cook partially, then add water to cover the tips, and boil briefly again.

—MICHEL GUÉRARD, adapted from
*Michel Guérard's Cuisine
Gourmand* (William Morrow)

900. When using a fish poacher, set the poacher over two burners on your stove.

—*Conventional kitchen wisdom*

901. Slide wooden spoons into the looped handles of a fish poacher insert to lift the cooked fish from the poacher. Place the fish on a large tray, undo the cheese-cloth, then use it to turn the fish from side to side for skinning.

—*Conventional kitchen wisdom*

902. An oval strainer makes a wonderful pasta scoop. It can be plunged to the bottom of the pot and its shape both captures and holds pasta.

—DEBORAH MADISON, adapted
from *The Savory Way* (Bantam)

903. A regular large wire sieve is perfect for sifting flour.

—*Conventional kitchen wisdom*

904. Sieves will last longer if you use the rounded bottom of a ladle rather than a spoon to force food through them.

—*Conventional kitchen wisdom*

905. If you have a good food mill, you can make to-mato sauce, apple sauce, and other purées without having to peel the fruits or vegetables. Sauces pick up

more color and flavor when cooked with the peel and are more nutritious, too.

—MICHAEL MCLAUGHLIN

906. Do not squeeze fresh tomatoes to remove the seeds because it makes them mushy. Instead, scoop the seeds out with a teaspoon.

—MARCELLA HAZAN

907. In a convenient kitchen drawer, keep a clear plastic 18-inch ruler marked with a grid. Use it to cut sheet cakes, bar cookies, or phyllo dough. It's perfect for drawing templates on parchment paper for special baking projects, measuring inscriptions for birthday and party cakes, etc.

—ALICE MEDRICH

908. Good-quality scissors that come apart for cleaning are invaluable for food preparation. Use them to cut chicken, pizza, bacon, pastry, and doughs as well as to snip herbs from their stems and open bags and boxes.

—JEAN HEWITT BLAIR

909. When cutting lady fingers or sponge cake to line a charlotte mold or other pan, use scissors instead of a knife. They're faster, neater.

—*Conventional kitchen wisdom*

910. When sharpening knives on a stone, lubricate with liquid dishwashing soap instead of machine oil

(toxic). The soap also floats away the steel particles so they can't clog the stone.

—JOHANNE KILLEEN and
GEORGE GERMON

911. The sharp open ends of clean cans make great biscuit, scone, and cookie cutters.

—JA

912. Needlenose pliers are great for debearding mussels and removing fish bones.

—LEAH STEWART

913. To coax morsels of crabmeat from deep crannies in the shell, try the handle of a teaspoon, a skewer, or a nut pick.

—DARINA ALLEN

914. Use wooden chopsticks for teasing ingredients out of the corners of the food processor or coffee grinder, for pushing a wad of wet paper towel around the bottom of a narrow jar or baby bottle to clean it, or for loosening hardened salt.

—ALICE MEDRICH

915. Use chopsticks for turning spaghetti in sauce, also for twirling it and eating it. Much easier than using a fork—*if* you know how to handle chopsticks.

—JULIA CHILD, adapted from a
segment on "Good Morning
America," ABC-TV

916. Use a wooden spoon to seed fruit rather than a metal one that might gouge the flesh.

—*Conventional kitchen wisdom*

917. Use a melon baller to seed cucumbers.

—DARINA ALLEN

ALSO

918. Use a melon baller to shape chocolate truffles and to core apples and pears.

—NANCY SILVERTON, adapted from *Desserts* (HarperCollins)

919. Use a grapefruit spoon or melon baller to clean the hairy choke from an artichoke.

—CALIFORNIA ARTICHOKE ADVISORY BOARD

920. Need to clean the intricate designs on fine silver? You'll find a mascara brush or toothbrush the perfect implement.

—JAMES BEARD, adapted from "The James Beard Show," "Cooking Classics," TV Food Network

921. Buy regular-bristle paint brushes to use as pastry brushes. Boil them to keep them clean.

—DIONE LUCAS, adapted from *The Dione Lucas Book of French Cooking*, with Marion Gorman (Little, Brown)

922. Use a funnel to drizzle oil into your blender when making vinaigrette or mayonnaise. It will fit right into the top of the blender.

—ALAN HARDING

923. The gadget to use for chopping eggs neatly and quickly? A pastry blender.

—JA

924. Use a thin-bladed knife, heated in a glass of hot water, to take smooth slices from a fresh goat cheese log. This helps prevent the cheese from crumbling.

—LAURA CHENEL

925. Use an ordinary wooden or plastic clothespin to seal bags of chips, packets of crackers, and cereal-box liners.

—TINA UJLAKI

926. The way to apportion chicken, macaroni, shrimp, or other cold salad quickly and equitably? With an ice cream scoop.

—JA

927. Also use an ice cream scoop to divide muffin or cake batter evenly in muffin tins.

—*Conventional kitchen wisdom*

928. Ever wonder what the numbers on ice cream scoops stand for? The number of scoops per quart.

—JA

929. Buy an inexpensive wooden dowel (about 18 inches long and 2 to 3 inches in diameter) and use in place of a rolling pin to roll over the edges of tart pans, trimming off excess dough. The tins' sharp metal edges will scar—and ruin—a good rolling pin.

—JIM DODGE, adapted from
Baking with Jim Dodge, with
Elaine Ratner (Simon &
Schuster)

930. The handiest container to use when decorating soups and sauces with "dots," "hearts," "pulled lines," and "cobwebs" is the kind of squirt bottle hairdressers use to apply hair color or waving lotion. The opening in the bottle tip is the perfect size for most designs, and can be snipped larger if you want bolder, broader strokes.

—ANNE WILLAN, adapted from
"Look & Cook" TV series, PBS
television.

931. Before chopping onions in the food processor, peel and quarter them and freeze for 30 minutes. This will minimize both mushiness and tears.

—MARLENE SOROSKY

932. With a food processor, you can make intensely flavorful vanilla sugar using fresh vanilla beans or ones you've already used to infuse a liquid. Rinse the beans, dry at room temperature or in a very low oven, and when brittle grind in your food processor with 2 cups of confectioners' (10X) sugar. You should have equal

weights of sugar and beans. Strain through a very fine mesh strainer to remove all crunchy bean bits. Use this vanilla sugar to dust cookies or to flavor whipped cream.

—NANCY SILVERTON, adapted from *Desserts* (HarperCollins)

933. Make your own superfine sugar by churning regular granulated sugar in a food processor or blender.

—ROSE LEVY BERANBAUM, adapted from *Cookies, Cakes & Pies* (Videocraft Classics, NYC)

934. Use your food processor to make fruit ices. Freeze the fruit mixture overnight in a shallow metal pan, then next morning put it in the processor and pulse until smooth, working in small batches. Refreeze and serve.

—MARIALISA CALTA

935. To chop or grind nuts fine in a food processor without turning them into nut butter, add 2 or more tablespoons sugar from the recipe.

—MARLENE SOROSKY

936. Put some bread through the roller of a new pasta machine or one that has not been used in some time to remove any oil or dust that may have accumulated inside. Repeat if necessary.

—JULIA DELLA CROCE, adapted from *Pasta Classica* (Chronicle)

937. A small electric coffee grinder can double as a spice grinder if you wipe it carefully before and after every use.

—*Conventional kitchen wisdom*

938. To caramelize the sugar on a dessert, use a chef's blowtorch. Also works for browning meringues.

—JULIA CHILD, adapted from *Julia Child & More Company* (Knopf)

CLEANUP

Easy Does It!

939. To simplify cleanup, switch to nonstick pans.

—JULIE DANNENBAUM

940. Clean as you work so dirty dishes don't pile up.

—JA

941. For quick wipe-ups of small spills, keep a box of plain white tissues near the stove and use them instead of paper towels.

—DIANA STURGIS

942. When cooking or using the food processor, proceed from "clean" foods to sticky. Saves on dishwashing, even dish rinsing.

—JACQUES PÉPIN, adapted from *The Short-Cut Cook* (William Morrow)

943. Avoid washing cast-iron pans whenever possible, wiping clean with a damp cloth, then drying thor-

oughly. If you must wash, use soap instead of a synthetic detergent. And always store uncovered lest beads of moisture collect and rust in the pan.

—JA

944. If you use water in cleaning your cast-iron pans, spray afterwards with nonstick vegetable cooking spray to prevent rusting.

—Jean Hewitt Blair

945. Never wash your cast-iron omelette pan. Use dry steel wool and a bit of oil to remove sticky bits.

—Dione Lucas, adapted from *The Dione Lucas Book of French Cooking*, with Marion Gorman (Little, Brown)

946. To brighten aluminum cookware, add 1 to 2 quarts water and 2 to 4 tablespoons cream of tartar and boil 5 to 10 minutes. Rinse, scour lightly with a steel-wool soap pad, then rinse again.

—*Conventional kitchen wisdom*

947. To clean copper pots, sprinkle well with lemon juice, then with salt, and rub with the cut side of a halved lemon.

—Martha Stewart, adapted from syndicated TV series, "Martha Stewart Living"

OR

948. While pots are still hot, drizzle with a little vinegar, sprinkle with salt, rub with a sponge, and rinse.

—JOHANNE KILLEEN and
GEORGE GERMON

949. Keep your prized copper beating bowl gleaming by scrubbing with a large pinch of salt, a squirt of vinegar, and a paper towel. Always clean it this way *before* you beat egg whites because the slightest bit of grease will keep the whites from whipping up properly.

—LEAH STEWART

950. Whenever practical, line baking pans with foil so they're a breeze to clean.

—JACQUES PÉPIN, adapted from
The Short-Cut Cook (William
Morrow)

951. Measures used for dry ingredients need only to be wiped thoroughly.

—SHIRLEY SARVIS

952. To clean automatic coffee makers, enameled cast-iron pots, and similar equipment, put 1 to 2 teaspoons of baking soda in the pot and pour boiling water over it. The dirt will peel right off. A baking powder solution is also great for scrubbing butcher blocks.

—SUSAN FRIEDLAND

953. Pans and dishes that have been used for mixing, beating, or cooking eggs [or milk or cheese] should be first rinsed with cold water, then washed with hot soapy water. A hot rinse "cooks" the eggs and makes things tougher to clean.

—JUDITH SEGAL

954. Fill dirty pots and pans with water as soon as you've finished cooking. Soaking loosens stubborn bits.

—JACQUES PÉPIN, adapted from *The Short-Cut Cook* (William Morrow)

AND

955. Add a little dishwasher detergent to make them soak clean faster.

—JA

956. To erase (or at least lessen) the white scum on fine crystal decanters, add about 1 cup white vinegar, stopper, and swirl to coat sides. Let stand briefly, swirl again, wash, rinse in hot water, and dry.

—JA

957. To clean a blender jar fast after making pesto or purée, squirt in a little detergent and fill halfway with water. Then frappé for 30 seconds and rinse out.

—REGINA SCHRAMBLING

AND

958. The same technique works like magic in a food processor.

—JA

959. If you use the same coffee grinder to grind both coffee and spices, clean it between uses by grinding up a piece of white bread, then wiping out the crumbs.

—SARA MOULTON

960. Never wash a pasta machine with soap or detergent or get water in it. Instead, wipe it with a slightly damp sponge. Dust between the rollers with a clean, dry pastry brush. Keep the machine covered between uses.

—JULIA DELLA CROCE, adapted
from *Pasta Classica* (Chronicle)

961. If something spills over in your oven, first sprinkle it with salt and remove with a metal spatula, then wipe with a damp sponge.

—JAMES BEARD, adapted from
"The James Beard Show,"
"Cooking Classics," TV Food
Network

962. A squirt of nonstick cooking spray can ease the pain of scrubbing barbecue grills, casseroles, roasting, and broiler pans. Always spray on cold grills.

—JEAN HEWITT BLAIR

963. Never wash a rolling pin (you may warp it). And never let dough dry on it. Immediately after rolling out dough, wipe the rolling pin clean with a towel and scrape off any stubborn bits with a plastic scraper.

> —JIM DODGE, adapted from
> *Baking with Jim Dodge*, with
> Elaine Ratner (Simon &
> Schuster)

964. Keep work surfaces clean by rolling dough between sheets of plastic wrap.

> —JACQUES PÉPIN, adapted from
> *The Short-Cut Cook* (William
> Morrow)

965. Before recapping bottles of syrup, molasses, oil, jams, and jellies, wipe the jar threads well with a damp cloth. Keeps bugs at bay and makes opening easier.

> —JA

966. Butter the pouring lip of a measuring cup or pitcher to prevent dribbling. Or spray the lip with nonstick cooking spray.

> —*Conventional kitchen wisdom*

967. Peel vegetables directly into the garbage disposal or trash can to simplify cleanup.

> —JACQUES PÉPIN, adapted from
> *The Short-Cut Cook* (William
> Morrow)

AND

968. Especially beets, which might stain the counter.

—CHARLES PIERCE

969. Wash your hands with lemon juice to remove beet stains.

—BERT GREENE, adapted from *The Vegetable Lover's Video* (Videocraft Classics, NYC)

970. After chopping garlic or onions, run a lemon quarter over both the knife blade and the cutting board to remove the odor.

—JESSICA HARRIS

971. A solution of 1 tablespoon baking soda to 1 quart warm water will remove most "off" odors from plastic storage containers. Simply give them a thorough dip in the soda solution, rinse with fresh water, and dry.

—BEN and KAREN BARKER

972. To deodorize a plastic storage container in which onions or garlic were stored, wash thoroughly, then stuff a crumpled piece of newspaper in the container, and snap on the lid. In a few days the smell will disappear.

—GILROY'S FINEST GARLIC

973. Place an open plastic bag near the telephone before you begin kneading dough or mixing meatloaf. When the phone rings (and it will), simply slip your hand in the bag before picking up the phone and avoid a sticky mess.

—ZANNE ZAKROFF

RECIPES

A Few Quickies & Homemade Convenience Foods

974. For easy summer hors d'oeuvre, put 1 tablespoon curry powder and 2 tablespoons salt in a plastic bag and shake to mix. Add, a few at a time, vine-ripe cherry tomatoes that have been rinsed and shaken almost dry. The remaining drops of water will make the curry mix stick to the tomatoes.

—MARY LYONS

975. Slice potatoes on a mandoline as thin as possible. Butter one side, press fresh herbs lightly into the butter, top with a second potato slice, and bake in 400° F. oven until crisp. The chips will fuse and become translucent, revealing the pattern of the herbs inside. Make ahead and reheat to use as a garnish or hors d'oeuvre.

—BEVERLY BARBOUR

976. Alternate stale bread chunks and fresh mozzarella cheese on skewers, brush with butter, and suspend

skewers on the edges of a roasting pan. Bake in a moderate oven until the bread is golden and crunchy, and the cheese begins to melt.

—CAROL FIELD, adapted from *Italy in Small Bites* (William Morrow)

977. Keep four to five different kinds of nuts in your freezer for drop-in guests. "Jump-fry" them in a hissing-hot nonstick skillet with a touch of butter, sea salt, and ground hot red pepper.

—ROZANNE GOLD

978. Make your own pita chips. Using scissors, separate the pockets into one layer by cutting around the circumference. Brush one side lightly with olive oil seasoned with crushed garlic and dried rosemary, or sprinkle with Parmesan, coarse salt, and ground hot red pepper. Stack the rounds and quickly, with a chef's knife, cut into pie-shaped wedges. Toast in a single layer on a cookie sheet in a 250° F. oven for 15 to 20 minutes until golden.

—MARIE SIMMONS

979. For a crustless quiche, butter a pie plate with 2½ tablespoons butter, then cover with toasted bread crumbs, pressing them firmly into the butter. Chill well in the freezer, fill with your favorite quiche filling recipe, and bake as directed.

—SIMONE BECK, adapted from *Food & Friends* (Viking Penguin)

980. Make quick soups for weekday lunches by mixing canned chicken and vegetable broth with bagfuls of preshredded carrots and coleslaw mix from your market's produce section. For a heartier version, add any leftover chicken or ham you may have on hand.

—BARBARA FAIRCHILD

981. Broil salmon à la Pacific Northwest on *untreated* cedar shingles bought at your local lumber store. Soak the shingles overnight, then warm briefly in the broiler to bring up the cedar flavor. Brush skinned salmon fillets with a mixture of salt, black pepper, dry mustard, and butter; place skinned side down on the cedar shingles; and broil 5 to 6 inches from the heat until the shingles scorch and the fish almost flakes—about 8 to 10 minutes. Serve on a bed of sautéed lettuce or greens.

—LARRY FORGIONE

982. To make your own convenience food: The next time you see ground beef on special, buy a lot. Get out the old stockpot and make a batch of Basic Meat Sauce. Freeze in serving-size portions and you're set for all kinds of quick meals that will save you time and money.

—MERLE ELLIS

BASIC MEAT SAUCE

Makes about 4 quarts

In an 8-quart stock pot, sauté 6 to 8 chopped medium-size onions and 3 to 4 chopped medium-size carrots in ¼ cup olive oil until limp but not brown. Stir in 2 to 3 tablespoons minced parsley and let it go a bit limp. Transfer all to a big bowl and set aside. Brown 5 pounds ground beef in the pot in 1½-pound batches, transferring to the bowl of vegetables. Add 1 (15-ounce) can tomato purée, 1 (8-ounce) can tomato sauce, and 1½ cups strong chicken stock or broth to the pot and stir to loosen the good stuff stuck to the bottom. Return everything to the pot and simmer, uncovered, about 30 minutes. Season to taste with salt and pepper. Cool to room temperature, then package in 2- or 3-cup freezer containers. Date, label, and freeze.

HOW TO USE BASIC MEAT SAUCE

983. For 15-minute spaghetti sauce: Cook ½ pound sweet or hot Italian sausage until lightly browned, crumbling with a fork as it cooks. Add ½ pound sliced fresh mushrooms and cook until limp. Mix in 4 cups Basic Meat Sauce, add 1 (28-ounce) can stewed tomatoes, 1 (6-ounce) can tomato paste, and 1 cup water. Season with 1 teaspoon each dried basil, rosemary, and oregano plus salt and pepper to taste. Cook down over high heat, stirring constantly, about 10 minutes or until sauce is the right consistency.

—MERLE ELLIS

984. For five-minute chili: Dump 2 (15-ounce) cans kidney beans into 3 cups Basic Meat Sauce, add 1 (6-ounce) can tomato juice and 3 tablespoons chili powder. That's it! Just heat through and serve with chopped onions.

—MERLE ELLIS

985. For the quickest chicken cacciatore ever: Top sautéed chicken with some of the Basic Meat Sauce, stewed tomatoes, sliced green peppers, and sliced pitted black olives and bring just to serving temperature.

—MERLE ELLIS

986. For Joe's Special: Scramble Basic Meat Sauce with fresh spinach, sliced fresh mushrooms, minced garlic, and eggs in a little garlic oil and you've got an easy adaptation of a specialty of the famous Joe's restaurants in the San Francisco Bay area.

—MERLE ELLIS

987. For Greek moussaka: Usually time-consuming, but a snap when you start with Basic Meat Sauce. Just add sliced eggplant and a little imaginative seasoning and bake until firm in a moderate oven.

—MERLE ELLIS

988. Wash and trim zucchini. If long, cut in thirds; if chunky, quarter lengthwise. Sprinkle with salt and pepper, dredge heavily with paprika and Parmesan, and dot with olive oil, if you like. Bake at 350° to

400° F. for 45 minutes to an hour—the longer you bake the zucchini without allowing it to burn, the better it will taste.

—NATALIE SCHRAM

989. Is there a perfect *Vinaigrette*? This one comes close: Combine ½ cup deeply fruity olive oil, 2 tablespoons red wine vinegar or freshly squeezed lemon juice (or 1 tablespoon of each), 2 teaspoons Dijon mustard, ¼ teaspoon salt and ⅛ teaspoon freshly ground black pepper in a shaker jar and shake vigorously until creamy. Makes about ¾ cup. Optional additions: ¼ teaspoon finely grated lemon zest and/or 1 finely minced garlic clove. Optional herbs: 1 teaspoon finely minced basil, chervil, chives, parsley *or* tarragon.

—*The chef's classic*

990. For a gutsy *Pesto Sauce*, choose the tips of about-to-bloom basil (they have more intense flavor than older, bigger leaves), then pack firmly into measuring cup. Here are the proportions for a quick processor *Pesto*: Churn 4 cups tightly packed tender young basil leaves and tips with 2 halved medium-size garlic cloves; 6 tablespoons room-temperature unsalted butter; ¼ cup *each* deeply fruity olive oil, lightly toasted *pignoli* (pine nuts) and freshly grated Parmesan; 2 tablespoons freshly grated Romano pecorino cheese and ¾ teaspoon salt for 60 seconds. Scrape down work bowl sides and continue processing until thick and smooth. Makes about 1 cup, enough for 4 servings.

—JA

991. If your homemade chicken broth seems wimpy, it may be the bird. Today's battery-raised poultry lacks flavor, so begin with an over-the-hill free-range hen. Load the pot with chunked vegetables: 2 large carrots (no need to peel), 2 large celery ribs (include tops), 2 large leeks (white part only), 1 quartered large yellow onion (no need to peel), ½ cup diced celery root, 2 to 3 large sprigs flat-leaf parsley. Add enough cold water to cover all by 1 inch. Simmer gently, uncovered, about 2 hours. Remove and reserve chicken for another use. Strain everything else through a colander lined with cheesecloth; discard solids. Skim off fat and season broth to taste with salt and freshly ground white or black pepper. Makes about 6 cups. *Note: If the broth still seems insipid, simmer uncovered until reduced by about a third. Or even easier, add a couple of chicken bouillon cubes.*

—JA

992. If you really want to pump up the flavor of chicken broth, brown the bird about 30 minutes at 400° F. before you add it to the stock pot—and leave the skin on. To boost the flavor still further (and also to enrich the color), substitute 1 cup canned vegetable juice for 1 cup of the water.

—Sandra Rose Gluck

And

993. Don't forget that turkey legs make terrific broth! Just substitute pound-for-pound for chicken.

—Sandra Rose Gluck

994. For good beef broth, always begin with plenty of raw bones (2½ to 3 pounds) and brown them well in the oven—about 30 minutes at 400° F. Pile in a stock pot along with ½ pound lean beef trimmings (also raw), 3 unpeeled large garlic cloves, 2 quartered large yellow onions (no need to peel), 2 large chunked carrots (no need to peel), 2 chunked large ribs celery (include tops), 1 cup diced celery root, 2 chunked large leeks, 4 large sprigs parsley and 2 quarts cold water. Simmer, uncovered, about 2 hours, skimming off the fat from time to time. Strain through a cheesecloth-lined colander and season to taste with salt and freshly ground black pepper; discard solids. If broth isn't strong enough, either boil down by about a third, or add a couple of beef bouillon cubes. Makes about 5 cups.

—The chef's classic

995. Try baking potatoes for your next batch of whipped potatoes. Scoop out the flesh, rice, then beat hard with salt, pepper, nutmeg, and just enough buttermilk to make them fluffy.

—GRAHAM KERR, adapted from
Graham Kerr's Smart Cooking
(Doubleday)

996. Cut up tomatoes, onions, and cucumbers for a summer salad, sprinkle with salt, and leave them in the bowl half an hour to give up their delicious juices. Blend these juices with the dressing for extra flavor.

—BARBARA KAFKA

997. Slice a red onion, add to boiling salted water, and blanch for 1 minute; drain and plunge into cold water. Drain again. Add 1 tablespoon sugar, 1 tablespoon white vinegar, and 3 tablespoons water. Cover and refrigerate. The onion is delicious spooned over a burger, added to tossed salad, or used as a relish.

—JAN T. HAZARD

OR FOR A REFRESHING VARIATION

998. Use a 50–50 mix of sliced red onion and cucumber.

—JEAN TODD FREEMAN

999. To make a deliciously mild vinegar, combine the peel of half a pineapple, a small chunk of pineapple flesh, ¼ cup dark brown sugar, and 1 quart water in a half-gallon preserving jar. Stir well, screw the lid on tight, then set in the sun. In a few days, when the mixture ferments, remove some of the peel. Gradually, as the liquid changes color and becomes more acid, remove the pineapple flesh and remaining peel. In 2½ to 3 weeks you'll have a pale, honey-colored vinegar. Strain and store in a cool, dark spot.

—DIANA KENNEDY, adapted from
The Cuisines of Mexico
(HarperCollins)

1,000. To make parsley oil, place one bunch of cleaned parsley and 3 cups olive oil in a container and let macerate overnight at room temperature. Next day blend the mixture in a food processor, strain, and bottle. Keep in the coldest part of the refrigerator and combine later with salt, pepper, and lemon juice for a flavorful salad dressing. Use within two weeks.

—GUY REUGE

1,001. A quick summer dessert for one: To ½ cup fresh blueberries add one small peach, peeled and sliced. Sprinkle with 1 teaspoon chopped crystallized ginger, toss gently, then dust with chopped fresh mint.

—MARY LYONS

The author gratefully acknowledges permission to quote or paraphrase from the following sources. Every care was taken to trace and secure all necessary permissions from copyright holders; however, if any have "slipped through the cracks," I apologize and will be happy to add any missing acknowledgments to subsequent editions.

A Fare for the Heart, A Cleveland Clinic Cookbook, Jacques Pépin, Chef. Copyright © 1988 by The Cleveland Clinic Foundation. Reprinted by permission of Jacques Pépin.

Anne Willan's "Look & Cook" Television Series, PBS Television; used by permission of Anne Willan.

Baking with Jim Dodge, published by Simon & Schuster. Copyright © 1991 by Jim Dodge with Elaine Ratner.

Better by Microwave by Lori Longbotham and Marie Simmons. Copyright © 1991 by Lori Longbotham & Marie Simmons. Used by permission of Dutton Signet, a division of Penguin Books USA, Inc.

The Complete Book of Kitchen Wisdom by Frieda Arkin. Copyright © 1968, 1977 by Frieda Arkin. Reprinted by permission of Henry Holt and Co., Inc.

Cooking Classics television series featuring Darina Allen's Irish Cooking Series, "Simply Delicious," "Simply Delicious for Family and Friends," and "Simply Delicious in Italy and France." Used by permission of Darina Allen.

Cuisines of Mexico by Diana Kennedy, published 1989, HarperCollins. Reprinted by permission of HarperCollins Publishers.

Desserts by Nancy Silverton, published 1991, HarperCollins. Reprinted by permission of HarperCollins Publishers.

The Dione Lucas Book of French Cooking by Dione Lucas and Marion Gorman, published 1973, Little, Brown. Reprinted by permission of Marion Gorman.

Food and Friends by Simone Beck. Copyright © 1991 by Simone Beck and Suzanne Patterson; line illustra-

Collins. Reprinted by permission of HarperCollins Publishers.

Ken Haedrich's Country Baking by Ken Haedrich. Copyright © 1990 by Ken Haedrich. Used by permission of Bantam Books, a division of Bantam Doubleday Dell Publishing Group, Inc.

La Cucina di Lidia by Lidia Bastianich with Jay Jacobs, published 1990, Doubleday. Reprinted by permission of Doubleday, a division of Bantam Doubleday Dell Publishing Group, Inc.

Madeleine Cooks Video Series, Volumes I and II, and *Madeleine Cooks Chicken,* by Breger Video, Inc. Permission of Breger Video, Inc.

Martha Stewart Living television series, used by permission of Martha Stewart.

Matters of Taste television series featuring Nathalie Dupree, used by permission of Nathalie Dupree.

Michel Guérard's Cuisine Gourmand by Michel Guérard. English translation copyright © 1979 by William Morrow & Company, Inc. Reprinted by permission of William Morrow & Company, Inc.

The Microwave Gourmet by Barbara Kafka. Copyright © 1987 by Barbara Kafka. Reprinted by permission of William Morrow & Company, Inc.

Pasta Classica by Julia della Croce. Copyright © 1987 by Julia della Croce. Published by Chronicle Books. Reprinted by permission of the Chronicle Books.

Paula Wolfert's World of Food by Paula Wolfert, published 1988, HarperCollins. Reprinted by permission of HarperCollins Publishers.

Rose's Christmas Cookies by Rose Levy Beranbaum. Text copyright © 1990 by Cordon Rose, Inc. Published 1990, William Morrow. Reprinted by permission of William Morrow & Company, Inc.

INDEX

Index

Index

Index

Index